BULGARIAN
PHRASE BOOK

DORLING KINDERSLEY PUBLISHING, INC.

DORLING KINDERSLEY PUBLISHING, INC.

LONDON • NEW YORK • DELHI • JOHANNESBURG
MUNICH • PARIS • SYDNEY

www.dk.com

Compiled by Lexus Ltd with Zhivko T Gulaboff
Language Consultant Dr Florentina Badalanova

First American Edition 2000
2 4 6 8 10 9 7 5 3 1

Published in the United States by Dorling Kindersley Publishing, Inc.
95 Madison Avenue, New York, New York 10016

Copyright © 2000 Dorling Kindersley Limited, London

Dorling Kindersley books can be purchased in bulk quantities at discounted
prices for use in promotions or as premiums. We are also able to offer special
editions and personalized jackets, corporate imprints, and excerpts from all of
our books, tailored specifically to meet your own needs. To find out more,
please contact: Special Markets Department, Dorling Kindersley Publishing, Inc.,
95 Madison Avenue, New York, NY 10016; Fax: 800-600-9098.

Library of Congress Cataloging-in-Publication Data
Bulgarian phrase book / [compiled by Lexus Ltd with Zhivko T. Gulaboff].
   p.   cm. -- (Dorling Kindersley travel guides phrase books)
Includes index.
ISBN 0–7894–5180–8 (alk. paper)
1. Bulgarian language--Conversation and phrase books--
English.   I. Gulaboff, Zhivko T. II. Lexus (Firm) III. Series.
PG839.B83 2000
491.8'183421--dc21
                                                        99–048549
                                                             CIP

Picture Credits
Jacket: special photography Stephen Shott bottom right and spine;
BRITSTOCK-IFA: Eric Bach, centre; CEPHAS: Mick Rock center left; ROBERT
HARDING PICTURE LIBRARY: top left, bottom center; Eye Ubiquitous: Bennett
Dean top right; POWERSTOCK: Rolf Richardson bottom left; POWERSTOCK/ZEFA:
back cover right; SCP: Sue Cunningham back cover left.

Printed and bound in Italy by Printer Trento Srl.

CONTENTS

PREFACE

This *Dorling Kindersley Travel Guides Phrase Book* has been compiled by experts to meet the general needs of tourists and business travelers. Arranged under headings such as Hotels, Driving, and so forth, the ample selection of useful words and phrases is supported by a 2,000-line mini-dictionary. There is also an extensive menu guide listing approximately 300 dishes or methods of cooking and presentation.

Typical replies to questions you may ask during your trip, and the signs or instructions you may see or hear, are shown in tinted boxes. In the main text, the pronunciation of Bulgarian words and phrases is imitated in English sound syllables. The Introduction gives basic guidelines to Bulgarian pronunciation.

Dorling Kindersley Travel Guides are recognized as the world's best travel guides. Each title features specially commissioned color photographs, cutaways of major buildings, 3-D aerial views, and detailed maps, plus information on sights, events, hotels, restaurants, shopping, and entertainment.

Dorling Kindersley Travel Guides titles include:

Amsterdam · Australia · Sydney · Berlin · Budapest · California
Florida · Hawaii · New York · San Francisco & Northern California
Canada · France · Loire Valley · Paris · Provence · Great Britain
London · Ireland · Dublin · Scotland · Greece: Athens & the Mainland
The Greek Islands · Istanbul · Italy · Florence & Tuscany
Milan & the Lakes · Naples · Rome · Sardinia · Sicily
Venice & the Veneto · Jerusalem & the Holy Land · Mexico · Moscow
St. Petersburg · Portugal · Lisbon · Prague · South Africa
Spain · Barcelona · Madrid · Seville & Andalusia · Thailand
Vienna · Warsaw

INTRODUCTION

PRONUNCIATION

When reading the imitated pronunciation, stress the part that is underlined. Pronounce each syllable as if it formed part of an English word, and you will be understood sufficiently well. Remember the points below, and your pronunciation will be even closer to the correct Bulgarian:

a	as in "far"
ay	as in "may"
e	as in "men"
ee	as the "ee" sound in "meeting"
g	always as in "go," not as in "German"
H	a guttural "ch" as in the Scottish word "loch"
I	as the "i" sound in "die"
j	as in "george"
o	as in "cod"
s	as in "sit"
u	as in "urgent," only shorter
zh	as the "s" in "leisure," only harder

The mini-dictionary provides Bulgarian translations in the form of the imitated pronunciation so that you can read the words without reference to the Bulgarian alphabet.

Over the page is a further guide to Bulgarian pronunciation, alongside the Bulgarian (Cyrillic) alphabet.

GENDERS AND ARTICLES

All Bulgarian nouns have one of three genders: masculine, feminine, or neuter. You can generally tell the gender of a noun by its ending:

most masculine nouns end in a consonant:
    eg. кон (*kon*) horse, стол (*stol*) chair;

most feminine nouns end in **-a** or **-я**:
  eg. жен**а** (*zhena*) woman, мас**а** (*masa*) table,
  ста**я** (*stia*) room;

neuter nouns end in **-e** or **-o**:
  eg. дет**е** (*deteh*) child, им**е** (*imeh*) name,
  палт**о** (*palto*) coat.

In Bulgarian, the definite article ("the") is not a separate word,
but an ending attached to the noun. This ending changes
according to the gender of the noun; the following will help
you create the definite form for singular noun endings.

There are two forms of the article for masculine nouns: the
short form and the full form. The full form is used only when
the noun is the subject of a sentence, but not in colloquial
spoken Bulgarian—when the short form is used in all
instances, whether or not the noun is the subject. You could
get by without using the full form.

a) masculine nouns add: **-a/-я**, (*-a/-ya*)
  eg. мъж (*mush*) man/a man, мъж**а** (*muzha*) the man;
  учител (*oochitel*) teacher/a teacher, учител**я** (*oochitelya*)
  the teacher.

b) masculine full form add: **-ът/-ят** (*-ut/-yat*)
  eg. мъж (*mush*) man/a man, мъж**ът** (*muzhut*) the man;
  учител (*oochitel*) teacher/a teacher, учител**ят** (*oochitelyat*)
  the teacher.

c) feminine nouns add: **-та** (*-ta*)
  eg. жена (*zhena*) woman/a woman, жена**та** (*zhenata*)
  the woman;
  маса (*masa*) table/a table, маса**та** (*masata*) the table.

d) neuter nouns add: **-то** (*-to*)
  eg. дете (*deteh*) child/a child, дете**то** (*deteto*) the child;
  име (*imeh*) name/a name, име**то** (*imeto*) the name.

There is no indefinite article in Bulgarian; for example, **жена** (*zhena*) can mean "woman" or "a woman." The word for "one" can be used for emphasis, but since this changes according to gender (**един мъж**, *edin mush*, "a man"; **една жена**, *edna zhena*, "a woman"; **едно име**, *edno imeh*, "a name") you'll probably avoid using it.

THE BULGARIAN (CYRILLIC) ALPHABET

letter		pronunciation
А	а	"a" as in "far"
Б	б	"b" as in "bag"
В	в	"v" as in "van"
Г	г	"g" as in "go"
Д	д	"d" as in "do"
Е	е	"e" as in "men"
Ж	ж	"zh" as the "s" in "leisure"
З	з	"z" as in "zoo"
И	и	"i" as in "bin"
Й	й	"y" as in "boy"
К	к	"k" as in "kin"
Л	л	"l" as in "lap"
М	м	"m" as in "mat"
Н	н	"n" as in "none"
О	о	"o" as in "cod"
П	п	"p" as in "pin"

letter		pronunciation
Р	р	similar to the Scottish rolled "r"
С	с	"s" as in "sit"
Т	т	"t" as in "tin"
У	у	"oo" as in "boot"
Ф	ф	"f" as in "fun"
Х	х	"ch" as in the Scottish word "loch"
Ц	ц	"ts" as in "let's"
Ч	ч	"ch" as in "chin"
Ш	ш	"sh" as in "shore"
Щ	щ	"sht" as in the end sound of "washed"
Ъ	ъ	"u" as in "urgent;" only shorter
Ь	ь	this softens the preceding consonant
Ю	ю	"you" as in "youth;" only shorter
Я	я	"ya" as in "yak"

The alternatives (*said by a man/woman*) in the phrases show the forms to be used by a male or female speaker.

USEFUL EVERYDAY PHRASES

Yes/No
Да/Не
da/neh

Thank you
Благодаря
blagodarya

No, thank you
Не, благодаря
neh, blagodarya

Please
Моля
molya

I don't understand
Не разбирам
neh razbiram

Do you speak English/French/German?
Говорите ли английски/френски/немски?
govoriteh li angleeski/frenski/nemski

I can't speak Bulgarian
Не говоря български
neh govorya bulgarski

I don't know
Не знам
neh znam

Please speak more slowly
Моля, говорете по-бавно
molya, govoreteh po bavno

Please write it down for me
Моля, напишете ми това
molya, napisheteh mi tova

My name is …
Казвам се ...
kazvam seh

How do you do, pleased to meet you
Здравейте, приятно ми е
zdravayteh, priyatno mi eh

Good morning
Добро утро
dobro ootro

Good afternoon
Добър ден
dobur den

Good evening
Добър вечер
dobur vecher

Good night *(when going to bed)*
Лека нощ
leka nosht

Goodbye
Довиждане
dovizhdaneh

Goodbye *(informal)*
Чао
chao

How are you?
Как сте?
kak steh

How are you? *(informal)*
Как си?
kak si

Excuse me, please
Извинете ме, моля
izvineteh meh, molya

Sorry! *(apology)*
Извинете!
izvineteh

Excuse me?
Моля?
molya

I'm really sorry
Много се извинявам
mnogo seh izvinyavam

Can you help me?
Бихте ли ми помогнали?
bihteh li mi pomognali

Can you tell me …?
Бихте ли ми казали …?
bihteh li mi kazali

May I have …?
Бихте ли ми дали …?
bihteh li mi dali

I would like … *(said by a man/woman)*
Бих искал/искала …
bih iskal/iskala

Is there … here?
Има ли тук …?
ima li took

Where can I get …?
Къде мога да намеря …?
kudeh moga da namerya

How much is it?
Колко струва?
kolko stroova

What time is it?
Колко е часът?
kolko eh chasa

I must go now
Трябва да си ходя
tryabva da si Hodya

I've lost my way
Изгубих се
izgoobiH seh

Cheers! *(toast)*
наздраве!
nazdraveh

Do you take credit cards?
Приемате ли кредитни карти?
priemateh li kreditni karti

Where is the restroom?
Къде е тоалетната?
kudeh eh toaletnata

Is there wheelchair access?
Може ли да се влезе с инвалидна количка?
mozheh li da seh vlezeh s invalidna kolichka

Are there facilities for the disabled?
Има ли приспособления за инвалиди?
ima li prisposobleniya za invalidi

Where is the US embassy?
Къде е Американското посолство?
kudeh eh amerikanskoto posolstvo

Go away!
Оставете ме на мира!
ostaveteh meh na mira

Excellent!
Чудесно!
choodesno

THINGS YOU'LL SEE

аварien изход	*avarien ishot*	emergency exit
асансьор	*asansyor*	elevator
Балкантурист	*balkantoorist*	Balkantourist
бутни	*bootni*	push
влезте	*vlesteh*	come right in
вода за пиене	*voda za pi-eneh*	drinking water
вход	*fhot*	entrance
вход забранен	*fhot zabranen*	no admittance
вход външни	*fhot za vunshni*	private, no
лица забранен	*litsa zabranen*	admittance
вход свободен	*fhot svoboden*	admission free
дава се под наем	*dava seh pod naem*	to rent
дръпни	*drupni*	pull
жени	*zheni*	women's
		restroom
заето	*zaeto*	occupied
запазено	*zapazeno*	reserved
затворено	*zatvoreno*	closed
изход	*ishot*	exit
изчакайте	*ischakiteh*	please wait
каса	*kasa*	cash register,
		cash desk
мъже	*muzheh*	men's restroom
отворено	*otvoreno*	open

→

работно време	*rabotno vremeh*	visiting hours, opening times
пазете тишина	*pazeteh tishina*	silence, quiet
пази се от боята	*pazi seh ot boyata*	wet paint
пожарен изход	*pozharen ishot*	fire exit
продава се	*prodava seh*	for sale
свободно	*svobodno*	vacant
сезонна разпродажба	*sezonna rasprodazhba*	sale
тоалетни	*toaletni*	restroom

THINGS YOU'LL HEAR

blagodarya	Thanks
blagodarya, dobreh —a vieh?	Very well, thank you —and you?
dovizhdaneh	Goodbye; See you later
izvineteh	Excuse me
kak si?	How are you? (informal)
kak steh?	How are you?
molya	You're welcome; Excuse me?
neh razbiram	I don't understand
neh znam	I don't know
taka li?	Is that so?
tochno taka	That's right
vnimavi!	Look out!
zapovyaditeh	Here you are
zdravayteh, priyatno mi eh	How do you do, nice to meet you

DAYS, MONTHS, SEASONS

Sunday	неделя	*nedelya*
Monday	понеделник	*ponedelnik*
Tuesday	вторник	*ftornik*
Wednesday	сряда	*sryada*
Thursday	четвъртък	*chetvurtuk*
Friday	петък	*petuk*
Saturday	събота	*subota*
January	януари	*yanooari*
February	февруари	*fevrooari*
March	март	*mart*
April	април	*april*
May	май	*mɪ*
June	юни	*yooni*
July	юли	*yooli*
August	август	*avgoost*
September	септември	*septemvri*
October	октомври	*oktomvri*
November	ноември	*noemvri*
December	декември	*dekemvri*
Spring	пролет	*prolet*
Summer	лято	*lyato*
Fall	есен	*esen*
Winter	зима	*zima*
Christmas	Коледа	*koleda*
Christmas Eve	Бъдни вечер	*budni vecher*
New Year	Нова година	*nova godina*
New Year's Eve	Новогодишна нощ	*novogodishna nosht*
Easter	Великден	*veligden*

NUMBERS

0	нула *noola*	16	шестнайсет *shesniset*
1	едно *edno*	17	седемнайсет *sedemniset*
2	две *dveh*	18	осемнайсет *osemniset*
3	три *tri*	19	деветнайсет *devetniset*
4	четири *chetiri*	20	двайсет *dviset*
5	пет *pet*	21	двайсет и едно *dviset i edno*
6	шест *shes*	22	двайсет и две *dviset i dveh*
7	седем *sedem*	30	трийсет *treeset*
8	осем *osem*	31	трийсет и едно *treeset i edno*
9	девет *devet*	32	трийсет и две *treeset i dveh*
10	десет *deset*	40	четирисет *chetirset*
11	единайсет *ediniset*	50	петдесет *pedeset*
12	дванайсет *dvaniset*	60	шейсет *shayset*
13	тринайсет *triniset*	70	седемдесет *sedemdeset*
14	четиринайсет *chetiriniset*	80	осемдесет *osemdeset*
15	петнайсет *petniset*	90	деветдесет *devedeset*

100	сто *sto*
110	сто и десет *sto i deset*
200	двеста *dvesta*
300	триста *trista*
400	четиристотин *chetiristotin*
500	петстотин *petstotin*
600	шестотин *shestotin*
700	седемстотин *sedemstotin*
800	осемстотин *osemstotin*
900	деветстотин *devetstotin*
1,000	хиляда *hilyada*
10,000	десет хиляди *deset hilyadi*
20,000	двайсет хиляди *dviset hilyadi*
100,000	сто хиляди *sto hilyadi*
1,000,000	милион *milion*

TIME

today	днес	*dnes*
yesterday	вчера	*fchera*
tomorrow	утре	*ootreh*
the day before yesterday	онзи ден	*onzi den*
the day after tomorrow	вдруги ден	*vdroogi den*
this week	тази седмица	*tazi sedmitsa*
last week	миналата седмица	*minalata sedmitsa*
next week	другата седмица	*droogata sedmitsa*
this morning	тази сутрин	*tazi sootrin*
this afternoon	днес следобяд	*dnes sletobyat*
this evening	тази вечер	*tazi vecher*
tonight	довечера	*dovechera*
yesterday afternoon	вчера следобяд	*fchera sletobyat*
last night	снощи	*snoshti*
tomorrow morning	утре сутринта	*ootreh sutrinta*
in three days	след три дни	*slet tri dni*
three days ago	преди три дни	*predi tri dni*
late	късно	*kusno*
early	рано	*rano*
soon	скоро	*skoro*
later on	по-късно	*po kusno*
at the moment	в момента	*fmomenta*
second	секунда	*sekoonda*
minute	минута	*minoota*
one minute	една минута	*edna minoota*
two minutes	две минути	*dveh minooti*
quarter of an hour	четвърт час	*chetvurt chas*
half an hour	половин час	*polvin chas*
three quarters of an hour	три-четвърти час	*tri chetvurti chas*
hour	час	*chas*

16

that day	този ден	*tozi den*
every day	всеки ден	*fseki den*
all day	цял ден	*tsyal den*
the next day	следващият ден	*sledvashtiya den*

TELLING TIME

To say "one o'clock," "two o'clock," etc., place the appropriate number in front of the word **часа** (*chasa*), meaning "hour." Some numbers in Bulgarian have different gender forms and the masculine forms for one and two are used for telling the time: "one o'clock" is **един часа** (*edin chasa*); "two o'clock" is **два часа** (*dva chasa*). The remaining hours up to twelve o'clock are simply the appropriate number plus the word **часа** (*chasa*).

For time past the hour, eg. "ten past five," Bulgarians say **пет и десет** (*pet i deset*), which translated literally means "five and ten." Sometimes you may hear the word **четвърт** (*chetvurt*) being used to denote a quarter of an hour—eg. "quarter past five" **пет и четвърт** (*pet i chetvurt*), but **пет и петнайсет** (*pet i petniset*), literally "five and fifteen," is more common. "Half past" is **и половина** (*i polovina*), literally "and half," or **и трийсет** (*i treeset*), "and thirty." So "half past three" can be either **три и половина** or **три и трийсет**.

For time to the hour, Bulgarians use **без** (*bes*), meaning "minus," so "quarter to" can be translated as **без четвърт** (*bes chetvurt*) or **без петнайсет** (*bes petniset*). "Quarter to five" is therefore **пет без четвърт** (*pet bes chetvurt*) or **пет без петнайсет** (*pet bes petniset*).

Minutes to the hour are expressed as in "quarter to …" above, eg. "five to three" **три без пет** (*tri bes pet*), literally "three minus five." All other expressions of time to the hour are formed following this pattern and there are no exceptions.

In general, the 24-hour clock is more commonly used than in the US, particularly on radio and TV.

The numbers section on page 15 provides the rest of the numerals necessary for telling time.

AM	сутрин	*sootrin*
PM	следобед	*sletobet*
one o'clock	един часа	*edin chasa*
ten past one	един и десет	*edin i deset*
quarter past one	един и петнайсет	*edin i petniset*
half past one	един и половина	*edin i polovina*
twenty to two	два без двайсет	*dva bes dviset*
quarter to two	два без петнайсет	*dva bes petniset*
two o'clock	два часа	*dva chasa*
13:00	тринайсет часа	*triniset chasa*
16:30	шестнайсет и трийсет	*shesniset i treeset*
at half past five	в пет и половина	*fpet i polovina*
at seven o'clock	в седем часа	*fsedem chasa*
noon	обед	*obet*
midnight	полунощ	*poloonosht*

HOTELS

Until recently, all hotels in which a foreigner was likely to stay were owned by the state tour operator Balkantourist. Although this company is currently being privatized, standards and arrangements remain much the same.

Hotels are classified as deluxe, first, second, and third category, or often (but not necessarily) with stars ranging from one to five. In city centers there is usually an Interhotel that conforms to the international standards for its category (normally between three- and five-star). Most other hotels, however, offer more than adequate accommodations for a fraction of the price that you would pay for an Interhotel room.

Many of the residences and vacation homes that were once reserved for party apparatchiks are now used as hotels and often provide more extras for the same price as Interhotels.

Most hotels in Bulgaria have at least one restaurant, bar, or coffee shop; larger hotels have more facilities such as room service, hairstyling, and shopping arcades.

The coastal resorts offer a variety of accommodations—conventional hotel complexes, purpose-built vacation villages (cottages and bungalows), and old towns with traditional Bulgarian architecture where you can stay in the newly emerging privately owned hotels or rent a private room. The latter often have the landlord or landlady living on the premises unless you rent a whole villa. Private rooms are usually excellent value for money and can be reserved at local tourist offices. Motels and campsites are to be found along the major tourist routes and the coast (see also Camping and Trailer Travel p. 26).

Breakfast may be included in the price of the room but this is much less common in Bulgaria than in the West and most likely only to be included with the room price in hotels with three or more stars. The prices for privately owned rented accommodations generally do not include breakfast.

Bulgarian bathrooms normally have only a shower; baths may be found in hotels with three or more stars. In any case, it is a good idea to take a universal bath/sink plug with you as this is the item most likely to be found missing even from luxury hotel bathrooms.

Hotel bills are usually expected to be settled in cash unless you are on a package vacation. Credit cards may be used in some big hotels and stores; this, however, is not always indicated clearly, and it is best to ask before you buy. Checks (with the exception of travelers' checks) are rarely accepted. The US dollar is the easiest foreign currency to pay with in Bulgaria; Western tourists are sometimes expected to pay directly in US dollars (although this is never obligatory). This, together with the variable exchange rate, makes it unwise to change large sums into Bulgarian currency at any one time. (See also Post Offices and Banks p. 83.) Tipping is at the usual rate of around 10%.

USEFUL WORDS AND PHRASES

balcony	балкон	*balkon*
bath (*tub*)	вана	*vana*
bathroom	баня	*banya*
bed	легло	*leglo*
bedroom	стая	*stja*
bill	сметка	*smetka*
breakfast	закуска	*zakooska*
dinner	вечеря	*vecherya*
double bed	двойно легло	*dvoyno leglo*
double room	двойна стая	*dvoyna stja*
elevator	асансьор	*asansyor*
full board	пълен пансион	*pulen pansion*
guesthouse	частен пансион	*chasten pansion*
half board	полупансион	*poloo pansion*
hotel	хотел	*hotel*
key	ключ	*klyooch*
lobby	фоайе	*fwa-yeh*
lounge	фоайе	*fwa-yeh*
lunch	обяд	*obyat*
maid	камериерка	*kameri-erka*

manager	управител	*oopravitel*
motel	мотел	*motel*
receipt	квитанция	*kvitantsiya*
reception	рецепция	*retseptsiya*
receptionist *(man)*	администратор	*administrator*
(woman)	администраторка	*administratorka*
restaurant	ресторант	*restorant*
room	стая	*stia*
room service	румсервиз	*roomservis*
shower	душ	*doosh*
single bed	единично легло	*edinichno leglo*
single room	единична стая	*ednichna stia*
sink	мивка	*mifka*
toilet	тоалетна	*toaletna*
twin room	стая с две легла	*stia zdveh legla*

Do you have any vacancies?
Имате ли свободни стаи?
imateh li svobodni sti

I have a reservation
Имам резервация
imam rezervatsiya

I'd like a double/twin room
Моля, дайте ми двойна стая/стая с две легла
molya, diteh mi dvoyna stia/stia zdveh legla

I'd like a room with a bathroom/with a balcony
Моля, дайте ми стая с баня/с балкон
molya, diteh mi stia zbanya/zbalkon

Is there satellite/cable TV in the rooms?
Има ли кабелна/сателитна телевизия в стаята?
ima li kabelna/satelitna televiziya f stiata

I'd like a room for one night/three nights
Моля, дайте ми стая за една нощувка/три нощувки
molya, diteh mi stia za edna noshtoofka/tri noshtoofki

What is the charge per night?
Колко струва една нощувка?
kolko stroova edna noshtoofka

I don't yet know how long I'll stay
Още не знам колко дълго ще остана
oshteh neh znam kolko dulgo shteh ostana

When is breakfast/dinner?
Кога е закуската/вечерята?
koga eh zakooskata/vecheryata

Would you have my luggage brought up?
Бихте ли изпратили багажа ми в стаята?
bihteh li ispratili bagazha mi fstiata

Please wake me at … o'clock
Моля, събудете ме в …
molya, suboodeteh meh f-

Can I have breakfast in my room?
Мога ли да поръчам закуска в стаята?
moga li da porucham zakooska fstiata

I'll be back at … o'clock
Ще се върна в …
shteh seh vurna f-

My room number is …
Номерът на стаята ми е …
nomera na stiata mi eh

I need a light bulb
Моля, сменете ми крушката
molya, smeneteh mi krooshkata

The lamp is broken
Лампата не работи
lampata neh raboti

There is no toilet paper in the bathroom
В банята няма тоалетна хартия
vbanyata nyama toaletna Hartiya

The window won't open
Прозорецът не се отваря
prozoretsa neh seh otvarya

The elevator/shower isn't working
Асансьорът/душът не работи
asansyora/doosha neh raboti

There isn't any hot water
Няма топла вода
nyama topla voda

I'd like to have some laundry done *(said by a man/woman)*
Бих искал/искала да оставя дрехи за пране
biH iskal/iskala da ostavya dreHi za praneh

The outlet in the bathroom doesn't work
Контактът в банята не работи
kontakta vbanyata neh raboti

I'm leaving tomorrow
Аз заминавам утре
as zaminavam ootreh

When do I have to vacate the room?
Кога трябва да освободя стаята?
koga tryabva da osvobodya stiata

May I have the bill, please?
Моля, дайте ми сметката?
molya, diteh mi smetkata

Can I pay by credit card?
Мога ли да платя с кредитна карта?
moga li da platya skreditna karta

I'll pay cash
Ще платя в брой
shteh platya vbroy

Can you get me a taxi?
Бихте ли ми поръчали такси?
biнteh li mi poruchali taxi

Can you recommend another hotel?
Бихте ли ми препоръчали друг хотел?
biнteh li mi preporuchali drook hotel

THINGS YOU'LL SEE

аварien изход	*avari-en isнot*	emergency exit
асансьор	*asansyor*	elevator
Балкантурист	*balkantoorist*	Balkantourist
баня	*banya*	bathroom
бутни	*bootni*	push
вана	*vana*	bath
втори етаж	*ftori etash*	third floor
вход	*fнot*	entrance
добавка	*dobafka*	supplement
дръпни	*drupni*	pull
душ	*doosh*	shower
гараж	*garash*	garage
закуска	*zakooska*	breakfast
Интерхотел	*interнotel*	Interhotel
мотел	*motel*	motel
нощувка и	*noshtoofka i*	bed and
закуска	*zakooska*	breakfast
няма свободни	*nyama svobodni*	no vacancies
легла/стаи	*legla/stı*	
обяд	*obyat*	lunch
офис	*ofis*	private
паркинг	*parkink*	parking lot

$\longrightarrow$

партер	parter	first floor
персонал	personal	staff only
полупансион	poloo pansion	half board
пълен пансион	pulen pansion	full board
първи етаж	purvi etash	second floor
резервация	rezervatsiya	reservation
ресторант	restorant	restaurant
рецепция	retseptsiya	reception
само за гости на	samo za gosti na	hotel patrons
хотела	Hotela	only
сметка	smetka	bill
стая под наем	stia pod naem	room for rent
сутерен	sooteren	basement
тоалетна	toaletna	toilet
частен пансион	chasten pansion	guesthouse

THINGS YOU'LL HEAR

suzhalyavam, no nyamameh svobodni legla
I'm sorry, we're full

nyamameh svobodni edinichni/dvoyni sti
There are no single/double rooms left

za kolko noshti?
For how many nights?

kak binteh zhelali da platiteh?
How will you be paying?

molya, plateteh predvaritelno
Please pay in advance

neh priemameh kreditni karti
We don't accept credit cards

tryabva da osvoboditeh stiata do dvaniset chasa
You must vacate the room by noon

CAMPING AND TRAILER TRAVEL

There are many campsites and camper (RV) sites in Bulgaria, and they are quite evenly distributed over the whole country with a number of them along the coast. Conditions and type of accommodations vary—from space on a lawn for a tent or a camper to the virtually hotel-like conditions of luxury tents or bungalows. All campsites and camper sites have restrooms, showers (there may be restrictions on the hot water availability), and kitchens or places for building a fire. Most sites will have a small grocery store or a stand for basic items and many will have at least a few market stalls where local people sell seasonal fruits and vegetables. Camping hardware like gas bottles, batteries, etc., however, is unlikely to be found for sale anywhere near the campsite—therefore buy all the hardware you need before you reach the site. Most campsites and camper sites close at the end of the summer. Camping rough and building fires in unauthorized places is illegal and punishable by an on-the-spot fine. Campsites are indicated on most Bulgarian road maps.

There are no specifically designated youth hostels in Bulgaria, but during the summer vacation some of the halls of residence **студентско общежитие** (*stoodentsko opshtezhitieh*) are used as youth hostels. You may be asked for an international student card before you are allocated a room. Places without student campuses may have basic accommodations in tourist dormitories **туристическа спалня** (*tooristicheska spalnya*), where you will be given a bunk in a large room that sleeps 15–20 people. Mountain chalets offer a similar type of accommodation, but a reservation from the Pirin Travel Agency in Sofia may be necessary.

USEFUL WORDS AND PHRASES

backpack	раница	*ranitsa*
bucket	кофа	*kofa*
camper (RV)	караван	*karavan*
camper site	къмпинг за	*kumpink za*

	караванани	*karavani*
campfire	лагерен огън	*lageren ogun*
campsite	къмпинг	*kumpink*
chalet	хижа	*Hizha*
cooking utensils	готварски пособия	*gotvarski posobiya*
cutlery	прибори за хранене	*pribori za Hraneneh*
drinking water	вода за пиене	*voda za pieneh*
flashlight	електрическо фенерче	*elektrichesko fenercheh*
garbage	отпадъци, боклук	*otpadutsi, bokloook*
hall of residence	студентско общежитие	*stoodentsko opshtezhitieh*
hitchhike	пътувам на автостоп	*putoovam na aftostop*
rope	въже	*vuzheh*
saucepans	тенджери	*tenjeri*
sleeping bag	спален чувал	*spalen choooval*
store	магазин	*magazin*
tent	палатка	*palatka*
tourist	туристическа	*toooristicheska*
dormitory	спалня	*spalnya*
trailer	ремарке	*remarkeh*

Can I camp here?
Мога ли да опъна палатка тук?
moga li da opuna palatka took

Can we park the camper here?
Можем ли да паркираме каравана тук?
mozhem li da parkirameh karavana took

Where is the nearest campsite/camper site?
Къде е най-близкия къмпинг/къмпинг за каравани?
kadeh eh nIbliskiya kumpink/kumpink za karavani

What is the charge per night?
Колко струва на вечер?
kolko stroova na vecher

I only want to stay for one night
Искам само да пренощувам
iskam samo da prenoshtoovam

Where is the kitchen?
Къде е кухнята?
kudeh eh koohnyata

Can I light a fire here?
Може ли да запаля огън тук?
mozheh li da zapalya ogun took

Where can I get …?
Къде мога да намеря ...?
kudeh moga da namerya

Is there any drinking water?
Има ли вода за пиене?
ima li voda za pieneh

THINGS YOU'LL SEE

душ	_doosh_	shower
забранено	_zabraneno_	forbidden
карта	_karta_	pass, identity card
кухня	_koohnya_	kitchen
огън	_ogun_	fire
опъването на палатки забранено	_opuvaneto na palatki zabraneno_	no camping
пропуск	_propoosk_	pass, identity card
студентско общежитие	_stoodentsko obshtezhitieh_	hall of residence
тоалетна	_toaletna_	toilet
туристическа спалня	_tooristicheska spalnya_	tourist dormitory
цени	_tseni_	charges, tariff

DRIVING

In the seventies, the Bulgarian government launched an ambitious building program designed to link the major cities—Sofia, Plovdiv, Bourgas, and Varna—with a circle of highways (named *Trakiya*, *Hemoos*, and *Cherno Moreh*) that would serve as the backbone of the road system in the country. Dogged by continuous cash crises, the project is still incomplete, although considerable parts of it have been built, notably the full length of the Sofia-Plovdiv highway, plus an extension covering most of the way from Plovdiv to the Turkish border in the direction of Istanbul. The Sofia-Varna highway, about a quarter of which is currently completed, covers the approaches to both cities. However, the country is adequately served by a good network of main roads (often with a third lane on the busiest stretches of road).

Rules of the Road: drive on the right, pass on the left. There are priority signs, but, in the absence of these, all secondary roads yield to major routes at intersections. In the case of roads having equal status or at unmarked intersections, the traffic coming from the right has priority. Note that in Sofia, trams coming from any direction have priority. Traffic circles are almost unknown in Bulgaria; all traffic is regulated by lights, but these are generally more visible than the ones in the US—with three sets employed on bigger city intersections: an eye-level set for the first driver in a line, a roadside set for medium-range visibility, and an overhead set for long-range visibility. You must not pass a tram that has stopped to allow passengers to get off. Both international and foreign driver's licenses are recognized. Civil liability insurance is compulsory and may be obtained at the border. The green insurance cards are valid. The current law does not allow for any amount of alcohol in the blood, so *do not drink and drive*.

The speed limit on highways is 75 mph (120 km/h) and on other main roads 50 mph (80 km/h); otherwise keep to the speed shown. Police speed traps are frequent on the main

roads and often unexpected. On-the-spot fines are always
levied for exceeding the speed limit. In built-up areas the limit
is 37 mph (60 km/h). A first-aid kit and a red warning triangle
in case of breakdown or accidents must be carried at all times.
Seat belts are compulsory.

Some gas stations on main routes and in the cities are open
24 hours a day, but elsewhere they close late at night. Allow
for at least 25 miles (40 km) between gas stations and possibly
more. Since some of them have recently been closed, long lines
may sometimes be necessary. Unleaded gas is available along
major routes and in most cities.

Fuel ratings are as follows:

leaded—супер (*sooper*)
diesel—дизелово гориво (*dizelovo gorivo*)
unleaded—безоловен (*bezoloven*)

SOME COMMON ROAD SIGNS

автоподлез	*aftopodles*	underground passage
включи фаровете	*fklyoochi faroveteh*	headlights on
влизането забранено	*vlizaneto zabraneno*	no entry, no tresspassing
внимание!	*vnimanieh*	caution
внимание влак	*vnimanieh vlak*	beware of the trains
внимание животни	*vnimanieh zhivotni*	cattle crossing
внимание пешеходци	*vnimanieh peshehottsi*	pedestrians
гараж!	*garash*	garage
гараж! не паркирай!	*garash neh parkiri*	garage— no parking
еднопосочно движение	*ednoposochno dvizhenieh*	one-way street
ж.п. прелез	*zheh peh preles*	train crossing

→

ж.п. преход	*zheh peh pr<u>e</u>not*	beware of the trains
изпреварването забранено	*isprev<u>a</u>rvaneto zabran<u>e</u>no*	no passing
карай бавно	*k<u>a</u>rı b<u>a</u>vno*	slow
край на магистралата	*krı na magistr<u>a</u>lata*	end of highway
лоша пътна настилка	*losha p<u>u</u>tna nast<u>i</u>lka*	bad surface
митница	*m<u>i</u>tnitsa*	customs
опасен завой	*op<u>a</u>sen zav<u>oy</u>*	dangerous curve
опасен кръстопът	*op<u>a</u>sen krustop<u>u</u>t*	dangerous intersection
опасност	*op<u>a</u>snost*	danger
отклонение	*otklon<u>e</u>nieh*	diversion
паркинг	*p<u>a</u>rkink*	parking lot
пешеходна зона	*pesh<u>e</u>н<u>o</u>dna z<u>o</u>na*	pedestrian area
първа помощ	*p<u>u</u>rva p<u>o</u>mosht*	first aid
път с предимство	*put spred<u>i</u>mstvo*	yield
ремонт на пътя	*rem<u>o</u>nt nap<u>u</u>tya*	roadworks
сервиз	*serv<u>i</u>s*	service station
училище	*oochil<u>i</u>shteh*	school
център	*ts<u>e</u>ntur*	town center

USEFUL WORDS AND PHRASES

brake (*noun*)	спирачка	*spir<u>a</u>chka*
breakdown	повреда	*povr<u>e</u>da*
car	лека кола	*l<u>e</u>ka kol<u>a</u>*
camper (*RV*)	караван	*karav<u>a</u>n*
clutch	амбреаж	*ambreh<u>a</u>sh*
engine	двигател	*dvig<u>a</u>tel*
exhaust	ауспух	*<u>o</u>wspoo<u>н</u>*
fanbelt	ремък	*r<u>e</u>muk*
garage (*for repairs*)	сервиз	*serv<u>i</u>s*
garage (*for gas*)	бензиностанция	*benzinost<u>a</u>ntsiya*
gas	бензин	*benz<u>i</u>n*

31

DRIVING

gear	скорост	*skorost*
gears	зъбни предавки	*zubni predafki*
headlights	фарове	*faroveh*
highway	автомагистрала	*aftomagistrala*
intersection (*highway*)	кръстовище	*krustovishteh*
	магистрален възел	*magistralen vuzel*
license	шофьорска книжка	*shofyorska knishka*
license plate	регистрационен	*registratsionen*
mirror	огледало	*ogledalo*
motorcycle	мотоциклет	*mototsiklet*
	номер	*nomer*
road	път	*put*
skid (*verb*)	занася се	*zanasya seh*
spare parts	резервни части	*rezervni chasti*
speed (*noun*)	скорост	*skorost*
speed limit	ограничение на скоростта	*ogranichenieh na skorosta*
speedometer	спидометър	*spidometur*
steering wheel	кормило	*kormilo*
taillights	стопове	*stopoveh*
tire	гума	*gooma*
tow	тегля	*teglya*
traffic jam	задръстване на движението	*zadrustvaneh na dvizhenieto*
traffic lights	светофар	*svetofar*
trailer	ремарке	*remarkeh*
truck	камион	*kamion*
trunk	багажник	*bagazhnik*
van	камионетка	*kamionetka*
wheel	колело	*kolelo*
windshield	предно стъкло	*predno stuklo*
windshield wiper	стъклочистачка	*stuklochistachka*

I'd like some gas/oil/water
Дайте ми бензин/масло/вода
diteh mi benzin/maslo/voda

Fill it up please!
Моля, напълнете резервоара!
molya, napulneteh rezervwara

I'd like 35 liters of gas
Дайте ми трийсет и пет литра бензин
diteh mi treeset i pet litra benzin

Would you check the tires please?
Бихте ли проверили гумите?
bihteh li proverili goomiteh

Do you do repairs?
Правите ли авторемонти?
praviteh li aftoremonti

Can you repair the clutch?
Можете ли да ремонтирате съединителната кутия?
mozheteh li da remontirateh suhedinitelnata kootiya

How long will it take?
Колко време ще отнеме?
kolko vremeh shteh otnemeh

Where can I park?
Къде мога да паркирам?
kudeh moga da parkiram

Can I park here?
Мога ли да паркирам тук?
moga li da parkiram took

There is something wrong with the engine
Има повреда в двигателя
ima povreda v dvigatelya

The engine is overheating
Двигателят загрява
dvigatelya zagryava

I need a new tire
Трябва ми нова гума
tryabva mi nova gooma

I'd like to rent a car
Искам да наема кола
iskam da naema kola

I'd like an automatic/a manual *(said by a man/woman)*
Бих искал/искала автоматичен модел/модел с ръчни
  скорости
bih iskal/iskala afttomatichen model/model sruchni skorosti

Is there a mileage charge?
Има ли такса на километър?
ima li taksa na kilometur

Where is the nearest garage?
Къде е най-близкият сервиз?
kudeh eh nibliskiya servis

How do I get to …?
Как да отида до …?
kak da otida do

Is this the road to …?
Това ли е пътят за …?
tova li eh putya za

THINGS YOU'LL HEAR

aftomatichen ili ruchen model iskateh?
Would you like an automatic or a manual?

diteh mi shofyorskata si knishka
May I see your license?

molya, dokoomentiteh
Please show me your documents

DIRECTIONS YOU MAY BE GIVEN

f<u>to</u>rata fl<u>ya</u>vo	second on the left
nad<u>ya</u>sno	on the right
nal<u>ya</u>vo	on the left
napr<u>a</u>vo	straight ahead
pokr<u>i</u> …	past the …
p<u>u</u>rvata vd<u>ya</u>sno	first on the right
zav<u>ee</u>teh nad<u>ya</u>sno	turn right
zav<u>ee</u>teh nal<u>ya</u>vo	turn left

THINGS YOU'LL SEE

безоловен бензин	*bezol<u>o</u>ven benzin*	unleaded
бензин	*benz<u>i</u>n*	gas
бензиностанция	*benzinost<u>a</u>ntsiya*	gas station
въздушно налягане	*vazd<u>oo</u>shno nal<u>ya</u>ganeh*	air pressure
дизелово гориво	*d<u>i</u>zelovo gor<u>i</u>vo*	diesel
глоба	*gl<u>o</u>ba*	fine
изход	*<u>i</u>sHot*	exit
колона	*kol<u>o</u>na*	line (of cars)
масло	*masl<u>o</u>*	oil
налягането на гумите	*nal<u>ya</u>ganeh na g<u>oo</u>miteh*	tire pressure
ниво на маслото	*n<u>i</u>vo na masl<u>o</u>to*	oil level
отбивка	*otb<u>i</u>fka*	detour
ремонт	*rem<u>o</u>nt*	repairs
сервиз	*serv<u>i</u>s*	garage for repairs
спирачна течност	*spir<u>a</u>chna t<u>e</u>chnost*	brake fluid
супер	*s<u>oo</u>per*	leaded gas

TRAVELING AROUND

AIR TRAVEL

Balkan Bulgarian Airlines operates scheduled flights between some US cities and the capital, Sofia. There is also a domestic network connecting the capital with the main Bulgarian cities along the Danube and the Black Sea coast. From Sofia, Balkan Bulgarian Airlines operates very competitively priced scheduled routes to many European, Middle Eastern, and North African capitals as well as to some Asian cities.

A visa is not required if you are planning to visit Bulgaria for less than 30 days.

TRAIN TRAVEL

Most towns and villages in Bulgaria are connected by the Bulgarian State Railways, initials **БДЖ**. The majority of Bulgarian trains may not be particularly fast or comfortable but they are reliable and inexpensive. Most cars are second class, but one or two per train will have first-class seats. Every main town in the country is connected to the capital by at least one express service **експресен влак** (*expresen vlak*) a day; most lines are serviced by a so-called fast train **бърз влак** (*burs vlak*), which is marginally slower and is supposed to stop only at larger-than-average stations. Small villages and branch lines are served only by the excruciatingly slow local trains **пътнически влак** (*putnicheski vlak*). Long-distance overnight trains between the major cities have between one and three sleeper cars (three- or six-berth compartments). Seats and berths should be reserved beforehand—ask for a reservation **запазено място** (*zapazeno myasto*). However, places on sleeper cars can also be bought from the sleeper car attendant on the night of travel. Larger cities may also have a Railroad Bureau **ж.п. бюро** (*zheh peh byooro*), usually situated in the city center, where you can buy tickets. Supplements, and sometimes fines, may be payable to the conductor on board if you take a faster train than stated on your ticket or wish to upgrade the class of your seat or berth.

Long-Distance Bus Travel

Even the tiniest village in Bulgaria can be reached by bus from the local center, which, in turn, will be served by buses to several of the major cities. Most towns have bus stations **автогара** (*aftogara*) where tickets are sold until about half an hour before departure. The state-owned bus company **Автотранспорт** (*aftotransport*) runs dilapidated and noisy buses to most destinations; tickets for these do, however, have the advantage of being sold at rock-bottom prices. Privately owned travel agents in bigger cities operate tourist-quality bus services to Sofia, Istanbul, and other destinations. Cross-border bus travel may be subjected to very long delays on the border crossings to Turkey and Romania.

Local Transportation

Bulgarian cities have good bus networks. Tickets for all state-run services (which are the majority) should be purchased in advance at one of the many kiosks and newsstands in the streets; they cost a few leva each and can be used for three types of transportation (bus, tram, and trolleybus) anywhere in the country; it is practical. therefore. to buy several at a time. The passenger must validate his/her ticket by punching it in the machine on board the bus, tram, or trolleybus. However, due to the increase in fare-dodging, some cities (like Varna) have reintroduced a conductor service. Many routes in the cities are served by privately operated minibus services with unspecified timetables (but they are fairly frequent during most of the day). On these the fare is paid to the driver.

TAXIS

The state-run taxi companies, which until a few years ago had a monopoly on the trade and were very hard to come by, are now competing with countless private taxis. All taxis display the sign **ТАКСИ**. Most of the private taxis do not have meters, and it would be wise to negotiate a price beforehand.

USEFUL WORDS AND PHRASES

adult	възрастен	*vuzrasten*
airport	летище	*letishteh*
airport bus	автобус до летището	*aftoboos do letishteto*
aisle seat	място до пътеката	*myasto do putekata*
baggage claim	получаване на багажа	*poloochavaneh na bagazha*
boarding pass	бордна карта	*bordna karta*
boat	кораб	*korap*
buffet	бюфет	*byoofet*
bus	автобус	*aftoboos*
bus station	автогара	*aftogara*
bus stop	автобусна спирка	*aftoboosna spirka*
car (*train*)	вагон	*vagon*
carry-on luggage	ръчен багаж	*ruchen bagash*
check-in desk	регистрация на багажа	*registratsiya na bagazha*
child	дете	*deteh*
compartment	купе	*koopeh*
connection	връзка	*vruska*
cruise	пътуване по море, круиз	*putoovaneh po moreh, kroois*
customs	митница	*mitnitsa*
departure lounge	зала заминаване	*zala zaminavaneh*
dining car	вагон-ресторант	*vagon-restorant*
dock	кей	*kay*
domestic	вътрешен	*vutreshen*

domestic arrivals	пристигане вътрешни линии	*pristiganeh vutreshni linee*
domestic departures	заминаване вътрешни линии	*zaminavaneh vutreshni linee*
emergency exit	аварен изход	*avarien ishot*
entrance	вход	*fHot*
exit	изход	*ishot*
fare	цена на билета	*tsena na bileta*
ferry	ферибот	*feribot*
first class	първа класа	*purva klasa*
flight	полет	*polet*
flight number	полет номер	*polet nomer*
gate	изход	*ishot*
international	международен	*mezhdoonaroden*
international arrivals	пристигане международни линии	*pristiganeh mezhdoonarodni linee*
international departures	заминаване международни линии	*zaminavaneh mezhdoonarodni linee*
lost and found office	бюро изгубени вещи	*byooro izgoobeni veshti*
luggage cart	количка за багаж	*kolichka za bagash*
luggage storage office	гардероб	*garderop*
minibus	микробус	*mikroboos*
nonsmoking	непушачи	*nepooshachi*
number 5 bus	автобус номер пет	*aftoboos nomer pet*
one-way ticket	билет	*bilet*
passport	паспорт	*pasport*
platform	перон, коловоз	*peron, kolovos*
port	пристанище	*pristanishteh*
railroad	ж.п. линия	*zheh peh lini-ya*
reservations office	бюро за билети	*byooro za bileti*
reserved seat	запазено място	*zapazeno myasto*

round-trip ticket	билет за отиване и въщане	*bilet za otivaneh i vrushtaneh*
seat	място	*myasto*
second class	втора класа	*ftora klasa*
ship	кораб	*korap*
underground passage	подлез	*podles*
sleeper car	спален вагон	*spalen vagon*
smoking	пушачи	*pooshachi*
station	гара	*gara*
taxi	такси	*taxi*
terminal (*bus*)	автогара	*aftogara*
ticket	билет	*bilet*
timetable	разписание	*raspisanieh*
train	влак	*vlak*
tram	трамвай	*tramvI*
trolleybus	тролейбус	*trolayboos*
visa	виза	*viza*
waiting room	чакалня	*chakalnya*
window seat	място до прозореца	*myasto do prozoretsa*

AIR TRAVEL

I'd like a nonsmoking seat, please
Място за непушачи, моля
myasto za nepooshachi, molya

I'd like a window seat, please
Място до прозореца, моля
myasto do prozoretsa, molya

How long will the flight be delayed?
Колко ще закъснее излитането?
kolko shteh zakusneh izlitaneto

Which gate for the flight to ...?
Кой е изходът за полета до ...?
koy eh ishoda za poleta do

Rail, Bus and Local Transportation

When does the train/bus for Sofia leave?
Кога заминава влакът/автобусът за София?
koga zaminava vlaka/aftoboosa za sofia

When does the train/bus from Varna arrive?
Кога пристига влакът/автобусът от Варна?
koga pristiga vlaka/aftoboosa ot varna

When is the next train/bus to Plovdiv?
Кога е следващият влак/автобус за Пловдив?
koga eh sledvashtiya vlak/aftoboos za plovdif

When is the first train/bus to Ruse?
Кога е първият влак/автобус за Русе?
koga eh purviya vlak/aftoboos za rooseh

When is the last train/bus to Burgas?
Кога е последният влак/автобус за Бургас?
koga eh posledni-ya vlak/aftoboos za boorgas

What is the fare to Istanbul?
Колко струва билетът до Истанбул?
kolko stroova bileta do istanbool

Do I have to change?
Ще трябва ли да сменям?
shteh tryabva li da smenyam

Does the train/bus stop at Gabrovo?
Влакът/автобусът спира ли в Габрово?
vlaka/aftoboosa spira li v gabrovo

How long does it take to get to Veliko Turnovo?
Колко време се пътува до Велико Търново?
kolko vremeh seh patoova do veliko turnovo

Where can I buy a ticket?
Къде мога да си купя билет?
kudeh moga da si koopya bilet

A one-way ticket to Sofia, please
Един билет до София, моля
edin bilet do sofia, molya

A round-trip ticket to Plovdiv, please
Билет за отиване и връщане до Пловдив, моля
bilet za otivaneh i vrushtaneh do plovdif, molya

Could you help me get a ticket?
Бихте ли ми помогнали да си купя билет?
bihteh li mi pomognali da si koopya bilet

Do I have to pay a supplement?
Трябва ли да платя добавка?
tryabva li da platya dobafka

I'd like to reserve a seat
Със запазено място, моля?
sus zapazeno myasto, molya

Is this the right train/bus for Vidin?
Това ли е влакът/автобусът за Видин?
tova li eh vlaka/aftoboosa za vidin

Is this the right platform for the Pleven train?
На този коловоз ли е влакъ за Плевен?
na tozi kolovos li eh vlaka za pleven

Which platform for the Sliven train?
На кой коловоз е влакът за Сливен?
na koy kolovos eh vlaka za sliven

Is the train/bus late?
Влакът/автобусът има ли закъснение?
vlaka/aftoboosa ima li zakusnenieh

Could you help me with my luggage, please?
Извинете, бихте ли ми помогнали с багажа?
izvineteh, bihteh li mi pomognali zbagazha

Is this a nonsmoking compartment?
Това купе за непушачи ли е?
tova koopeh za nepooshachi li eh

Is this seat free?
Свободно ли е това място?
svobodno li eh tova myasto

This seat is taken
Това място е заето
tova myasto eh zaheto

I have reserved this seat
Това е моето запазено място
tova eh moeto zapazeno myasto

May I open/close the window?
Може ли да отворя/затворя прозореца?
mozheh li da otvorya/zatvorya prozoretsa

When do we arrive in Kazanluk?
Кога пристигаме в Казанлък?
koga pristigameh fkazanluk

What station is this?
Коя е тази гара?
koya eh tazi gara

Do we stop at Kaprivshtitsa?
Влакът спира ли в Копривщица?
vlaka spira li v koprifshtitsa

Is there a dining car on this train?
Има ли вагон-ресторант във влака?
ima li vagon-restorant vuf vlaka

Where is the bus station?
Къде е автогарата?
kudeh eh aftogarata

Where is there a bus stop?
Къде има спирка?
kudeh ima spirka

Which buses go to Nesebar?
Кои автобуси отиват до Несебър?
kwi aftoboosi otivat do nesebur

How often do the buses to Golden Sands run?
На колко време са автобусите до Златните Пясъци?
na kolko vremeh sa aftoboositeh do zlatniteh pyasutsi

Will you let me know when we're there?
Бихте ли ми казали когато стигнем дотам?
bihteh li mi kazali kogato stignem dotam

Do I have to get off yet?
Тук ли трябва да сляза?
took li tryabva da slyaza

How do you get to Varna city center?
Как се отива до центъра на Варна?
kak seh otiva do tsentura na varna

Do you go near the city center?
Минавате ли покрай центъра на града?
minavateh li pokri tsentura na grada

I want to go to the Rila Monastery
Искам да отида до Рилския манастир
iskam da otida do rilskiya manastir

TAXI

Where can I get a taxi?
Къде мога да взема такси?
kudeh moga da vzema taxi

To the airport, please
До летището, моля
do letishteto, molya

I'll give you 150 leva
Ще ви дам сто и петдесет лева
shteh vi dam sto i pedeset leva

Please stop here
Спрете тук, моля
spreteh took, molya

I'd like a receipt, please
Бихте ли ми дали квитанция?
bihteh li mi dali kvitantsiya

I would like you to wait here for me and take me back
Ще ви помоля да ме изчакате тук и да ме върнете обратно
shteh vi pomolya da meh ischakateh took idameh vurneteh obratno

Keep the change
Задръжте рестото
zadrushteh restoto

THINGS YOU'LL SEE

аварien изход	avar<u>ie</u>n <u>i</u>sнot	emergency exit
аварийна сигнализация	avar<u>ee</u>na signaliz<u>a</u>tsiya	emergency stop cord
Автотранспорт	aftotransp<u>o</u>rt	state-owned bus company
автобус за летището	aftob<u>oo</u>s za let<u>i</u>shteto	airport bus
автогара	<u>a</u>ftog<u>a</u>ra	terminal (bus)
Балкан	balk<u>a</u>n	Bulgarian Airlines
БДЖ	beh-deh-zheh	Bulgarian State Railways
билети	bil<u>e</u>ti	tickets, ticket office
билетна каса	bil<u>e</u>tna k<u>a</u>sa	ticket office
бордна карта	b<u>o</u>rdna k<u>a</u>rta	boarding pass
бърз влак	burz vlak	fast train
бюро за билети	byoor<u>o</u> za bil<u>e</u>ti	reservations office
вагон	vag<u>o</u>n	car (train)
вход	fнot	entrance
вход забранен	fнot zabran<u>e</u>n	no entry
вход от другата страна	fнot ot dr<u>oo</u>gata stran<u>a</u>	enter from the other side
възрастни	v<u>u</u>zrastni	adults
вътрешни линии	v<u>u</u>treshni l<u>i</u>nee	domestic (flights)
гардероб	garder<u>o</u>p	luggage storage office
деца	dets<u>a</u>	children
директен полет	dir<u>e</u>kten p<u>o</u>let	direct flight
добавка	dob<u>a</u>fka	supplement
експресен влак	ekspr<u>e</u>sen vlak	express train
жени	zhen<u>i</u>	women
ж.п. бюро	zheh peh byoor<u>o</u>	Railway Bureau
заето	za<u>e</u>to	occupied
закуски	zak<u>oo</u>ski	snacks
закъснение	zakusn<u>e</u>nieh	delay

→

46

заминаване	*zamin<u>a</u>vaneh*	departures
запазено място	*zap<u>a</u>zeno m<u>ya</u>sto*	reserved seat
изход	*<u>i</u>shot*	exit, gate
изход към пероните	*<u>i</u>shot kum per<u>o</u>niteh*	to the trains
информация	*inform<u>a</u>tsiya*	information
маршрут	*marshr<u>oo</u>t*	route
международни линии	*mezhdoonar<u>o</u>dni l<u>i</u>nee*	international (flights)
места	*mest<u>a</u>*	seats
местно време	*m<u>e</u>stno vr<u>e</u>meh*	local time
митнически контрол	*m<u>i</u>tnicheski kontr<u>o</u>l*	customs control
мъже	*muzh<u>e</u>h*	men
нарушителите се глобяват	*naroosh<u>i</u>teliteh seh glob<u>ya</u>vat*	penalty for misuse
не говорете с водача	*neh govor<u>e</u>teh zvod<u>a</u>cha*	do not speak to the driver
неделя и почивни дни	*ned<u>e</u>lya i poch<u>i</u>vni dni*	Sundays and public holidays
непушачи	*nepoosh<u>a</u>chi*	nonsmoking
не се навеждай навън	*neh seh nav<u>e</u>zhdı navun*	do not lean out of the window
не спира в ...	*ne sp<u>i</u>ra v ...*	does not stop in ...
обмяна на валута	*obm<u>ya</u>na na val<u>oo</u>ta*	currency exchange
паспортен контрол	*pasp<u>o</u>rten kontr<u>o</u>l*	passport control
перон	*per<u>o</u>n*	platform
плащам	*pl<u>a</u>shtam*	to pay
полет	*pol<u>e</u>t*	flight
получаване на багажа	*polooch<u>a</u>vaneh na bag<u>a</u>zha*	baggage claim
пристанище	*prist<u>a</u>nishteh*	harbor
пристигане	*prist<u>i</u>ganeh*	arrivals
пушачи	*poosh<u>a</u>chi*	smoking

→

47

пушенето забранено	*poosheneto zabraneno*	no smoking
пътнически влак	*putnicheski vlak*	local train
пътници	*putnitsi*	passengers
пътуване	*putoovaneh*	trip
разписание	*raspisanieh*	timetable
регистрация	*registratsiya*	check-in
редовен полет	*redoven polet*	scheduled flight
РЕП	*rep*	newsstand
само в работни дни	*samo frabotni dni*	weekdays only
свободно	*svobodno*	vacant
смяна в ...	*smyana v ...*	change at ......
спирка	*spirka*	stop
станция за таксита	*stantsiya za taksita*	taxi stand
такси	*taxi*	taxi
тоалетна	*toaletna*	toilet
централна гара	*tsentralna gara*	central station
чакалня	*chakalnya*	waiting room

THINGS YOU'LL HEAR

imateh li bagash?
Do you have any luggage?

pooshachi ili nepooshachi?
Smoking or nonsmoking?

myasto do prozoretsa ili do putekata?
Window seat or aisle seat?

purvo povikvaneh na putnitsiteh za ...
The flight for ... is now boarding

vnimanieh
Attention

→

molya biletiteh
Tickets, please

kacheteh seh na vlaka
Board the train

vlakut za ... shteh zamineh ot ... kolovos v ... chasa
The train for ... will leave from platform ... at ...

vlak nomer ... shteh pristigneh na ... kolovos v ... chasa
Train number ... will arrive at platform ... at ...

vlak nomer ... seh dvizhi sus ... minooti zakusnenieh
Train number ... is ... minutes late

vashi-ya pasport, molya
Your passport, please

molya otvoreteh koofariteh
Open your suitcases, please

imateh li neshto za deklariraneh?
Do you have anything to declare?

REPLIES YOU MAY BE GIVEN

sledvashtiya vlak zaminava v ...
The next train leaves at ...

smyana v ...
Change at ...

tryabva da platiteh dobafka
You must pay a supplement

nyama svobodni mesta za ...
There are no more seats available for ...

EATING OUT

Like most of the hotels, the majority of restaurants **ресторант** (*restorant*) in Bulgaria used to be owned by the state-run tourist company Balkantourist. This has imposed a certain uniformity in design and choice of food. Although categories exist, they are not clearly indicated but can be easily guessed once you have had a look at the place. Restaurants are usually open between 11 AM–2 PM and 6 PM–11 PM daily.

Waiter-service restaurants fall roughly into two kinds: "international" and folk-style. Both types can offer high-quality or mediocre food, although the majority will have something in between. Finding out about each place in particular is very much a matter of trial and error.

More specifically, the kinds of eating places in Bulgaria are:

Waiter-service restaurants:
- hotel and main street restaurants: good quality international cuisine, if slightly pricier than average;
- **ханче** (*hancheh*) or **механа** (*mehana*): Bulgarian folk restaurants providing home-style cooking served in a 19th century folk-style environment (waiters in national dress, etc.).

Self-service restaurants:
- **закусваля** (*zakoosvalnya*) cafeteria: unlicensed and inexpensive but rarely very clean. They sell snacks as well as soups and hot dishes.
- **скара-бира** (*skara-bira*) grill and beer joints: rough-and-ready shed-type affairs with tables outside where the burger-style meats are barbecued as you wait and are then traditionally washed down with Bulgarian beer. This fare is incidentally what Bulgarians excel in making and consuming. It is well worth trying if you want to find out about the flavor of local life.

Ethnic restaurants are mostly found in Sofia, with some Chinese and Vietnamese, European, and Mexican cooking represented, but don't be surprised if the dishes differ slightly from what you are used to since they will be made from mostly local ingredients.

There should be plenty of choice available for vegetarians, but it is probably best to ask whether a dish you are interested in contains meat or fish since you are unlikely to find specifically vegetarian menus.

In bigger cities and package resorts there are variety restaurants that stage entertainment of, for example, a Bulgarian wedding, gypsy and shepherd rituals, dancing on hot coals, etc.

Drinking places have increased both in number and in variety since the end of the ban on private enterprise. Most of these are called **кафе-аператив** (*kafeh-aperitif*) and offer local and imported liquor, soft drinks, and sometimes ice cream. You might also like to try some of Bulgaria's excellent, and inexpensive, local wines. Drinking places usually have waiter-service and the service can be slow. Smoking is allowed in all licensed establishments and ventilation is rarely good, so finding an outside table is always the best option. Older Bulgarians tend to use restaurants for social drinking; the younger drinkers prefer the *kafeh-aperitif* bars. Western-style bars exist in most hotels and are generally known as **дневен бар** *dneven bar*) "day-bar" (open 11 AM–11 PM) as opposed to the **нощен бар** (*noshten bar*) "night bar" or "nightclub" establishments, mostly to be found in the more upscale hotels —these are variety clubs with a floor show and are open between 10 PM and 4 AM.

Another popular catering establishment often seen in Bulgaria is the café-pâtisserie—**сладкарница** (*slatkarnitsa*). Its main fare is a selection of syrupy cakes and cream cakes, toasted sandwiches, ice creams, and non-alcoholic hot and cold drinks. They are only licensed if they are in a hotel and double as day-bars.

Probably the best place to have breakfast in Bulgaria is one of the small street bakeries that churn out hot cheese-filled pastries **баничка** (*banichka*), marmalade-filled sweet rolls **кифла** (*kifla*), and bagels **геврек** (*gevrek*) all day long. These bakeries do not sell anything else or have tables—the only option being to eat on the run, which is quite acceptable in Bulgaria.

USEFUL WORDS AND PHRASES

beer	бира	*bira*
bottle	бутилка	*bootilka*
cake	паста	*pasta*
check	сметка	*smetka*
chef	майстор-готвач	*mistor-gotvach*
coffee	кафе	*kafeh*
cup	чаша	*chasha*
fork	вилица	*vilitsa*
glass	чаша	*chasha*
knife	нож	*nosh*
menu	меню	*menyoo*
milk	мляко	*mlyako*
napkin	салфетка	*salfetka*
plate	чиния	*chiniya*
receipt	касова бележка	*kasova beleshka*
sandwich	сандвич	*sandvich*
snack	закуска	*zakooska*
soup	супа	*soopa*
spoon	лъжица	*luzhitsa*
sugar	захар	*zahar*
table	маса	*masa*
tea	чай	*chi*
teaspoon	лъжичка	*luzhichka*
tip	бакшиш	*bakshish*
waiter	сервитьор	*servityor*
waitress	сервитьорка	*servityorka*
water	вода	*voda*
wine	вино	*vino*
wine list	меню за напитки	*menyoo za napitki*

A table for one, please
Маса за един, моля
masa za edin, molya

A table for two, please
Маса за двама, моля
masa za dvama, molya

Is there a highchair?
Има ли детски столчета с масичка за хранене?
ima li detski stolcheta s masichka za hraneneh

May I see the menu?
Бихте ли ми дали менюто, моля?
bihteh li mi dali menyooto

May I see the wine list?
Бихте ли ми дали менюто за напитки?
bihteh li mi dali menyooto za napitki

What would you recommend?
Какво ще ми препоръчате?
kakvo shteh mi preporuchateh

Do you do children's portions?
Имате ли детски порции?
imateh li detski portsii

Can you warm this bottle/baby food for me?
Може ли да затоплите бутилката/бебешката храна?
mozheh li da zatopliteh bootilkata/bebeshkata hrana

I'd like …
Моля, дайте ми ...
molya, diteh mi

Is this suitable for vegetarians?
Подходящо ли е за вегетарианци?
podhodyashto li eh za vegetariantsi

Just a cup of coffee/tea, please
Само едно кафе/чай, моля
samo edno kafeh/chi, molya

I'm allergic to nuts/shellfish
Имам алергия към ядки/стриди и раци
imam alergiya kum yadki/stridi i ratsi

Waiter/waitress!
Моля! Келнер!
molya, kelner

May we have the check, please?
Моля, сметката!
molya, smetkata

I only want a snack *(said by a man/woman)*
Бих искал/искала само лека закуска
bih iskal/iskala samo leka zakooska

I didn't order this
Аз не поръчах това
as neh poruchah tova

May we have some more …?
Бихте ли донесли още ...?
bihteh li donesli oshteh

The meal was very good, thank you
Яденето беше чудесно, благодаря
yadeneto besheh choodesno, blagodarya

My compliments to the chef!
Благодарете на майстора от мое име!
blagodareteh na mistora ot moeh imeh

I think there is a mistake on the check
Струва ми се, че има грешка в сметката
stroova mi seh, cheh ima greshka fsmetkata

Things You'll Hear

dobur apetit!
Enjoy your meal!

kakvo shteh zhelaeteh?
What would you like?

binteh li zhelali oshteh …?
Would you like some more …?

nyamameh svobodni masi
We have no free tables

nyamameh …
We don't have any …

Things You'll See

бирария	*birariya*	beer and grills joint, bar
гардероб	*garderop*	cloakroom
гардеробът е задължителен	*garderobut eh zadulzhitelen*	cloakroom obligatory
каса	*kasa*	pay here
кафе	*kafeh*	coffee shop
кухня	*koohnya*	kitchens
ресторант	*restorant*	restaurant
офис	*ofis*	kitchens
самообслужване	*samo-opsloozhivaneh*	self-service
тоалетна	*toaletna*	restroom

MENU GUIDE

STARTERS

гъби с масло *gubi smaslo*	mushrooms fried in butter
език пане *ezik paneh*	fried tongue in batter
жабешки бутчета *zhabeshki bootcheta*	frog's legs
картофи със сирене *kartofi sus sireneh*	french fries with feta cheese
кашкавал *kashkaval*	hard yellow cheese
кашкавал пане *kashkaval paneh*	fried yellow cheese in batter
кьополу *kyopoloo*	chopped baked eggplant and peppers with tomatoes and garlic in vinaigrette
луканка *lookanka*	long, flat, dry-cured, spicy sausage, served in thin slices
маслини с лук *maslini slook*	olives with onion
миди *midi*	mussels
мозък пане *mozuk paneh*	fried brains in batter
омлет със сирене *omlet sus sireneh*	cheese omelette
омлет по градинарски *omlet po gradinarski*	vegetable omelette
охлюви *ohlyoovi*	snails
патлажан бюрек *patlajan byoorek*	fried eggplant stuffed with cheese paste
сирене *sireneh*	feta cheese
суджук *soojook*	horseshoe-shaped, dry-cured sausage, similar to *lookanka*
тиквичка бюрек *tikvichka byoorek*	fried zucchini stuffed with cheese paste
тиквички пържени *tikvichki purzheni*	fried sliced zucchini
филе *fileh*	dry-cured, spicy pork or venison fillet, served in thin slices
хеменедекс *hemendeks*	ham and eggs
червен хайвер *cherven HIver*	red caviar
черен хайвер *cheren HIver*	caviar
чушка бюрек *chooshka byoorek*	fried pepper stuffed with cheese paste and eggs
чушки пържени *chooshki purzheni*	fried peppers
шкембе в гювече *shkembeh vgyoovecheh*	tripe stew, made in an earthenware pot
шпеков салам *shpekof salam*	salami

SALADS

варен боб с лук *varen bop slook*
бean salad with onion

домати *domati*
tomatoes

домати със сирене *domati sus sireneh*
tomatoes with feta cheese

зеле *zeleh*
raw, finely chopped cabbage

зелена салата *zelena salata*
salad of lettuce, spring onions
and radishes

картофи с лук *kartofi slook*
potato salad with onion

краставици *krastavitsi*
cucumbers

мешана *meshana*
tomatoes and cucumbers

мешана с лук *meshana slook*
tomatoes, cucumbers, and onion

руска *rooska*
Russian salad (potatoes, peas,
ham, pickles, boiled eggs—
chopped and mixed with
mayonnaise)

чушки *chooshki*
baked peppers served cold
in vinaigrette

шопска *shopska*
tomatoes, cucumber, onion,
peppers, parsley, and feta
cheese

SOUPS

градинарска чорба *gradinarska chorba*
mixed vegetable soup

гулаш *goolash*
goulash soup—made with
vegetables, pulses, and paprika

крем-супа от домати *krem-soopa ot domati*
cream of tomato soup

курбан чорба *koorban chorba*
lamb soup with rice

манастирска чорба *manastirska chorba*
white bean and vegetable soup

супа от спанак *soopa ot spanak*
spinach soup

супа от леща *soopa ot leshta*
lentil soup

супа топчета *soopa topcheta*
soup with meatballs

таратор *tarator*
cold soup made from chopped
cucumber, yogurt, garlic, dill
and walnuts

телешко варено *teleshko vareno*
veal and vegetables in clear
bouillon

шкембе чорба *shkembeh chorba*
tripe soup

MENU GUIDE

MEAT DISHES

агнешка дроб-сърма *agneshka dropsarma* — spicy lamb and lamb offal roasted in caul parcels

винен кебап *vinen kebap* — pork stewed in wine

гювеч *gyoovech* — pork and vegetable stew baked in an earthenware dish called a *gyoovech*; contains peppers, tomatoes, onions, eggplant, okra, potatoes, parsley

дивеч *divech* — game

домашна наденица *domashna nadenitsa* — Bulgarian pork and beef sausage

задушено пиле *zadoosheno pileh* — chicken stewed with vegetables

карета *kareta* — grilled pork fillets

кърначета *karnacheta* — thin, round, grilled Bulgarian sausage

кебапчета *kebapcheta* — grilled oblong rissoles

кюфтета *kyoofteta* — grilled meatballs

мешана скара *meshana skara* — mixed grill of pork fillet, *kebapcheh*, large meatball, pork on a skewer, round sausage, and often mushrooms

мусака *moosaka* — moussaka — layers of ground meat, potatoes, eggplant, and tomatoes, topped with a white sauce made with eggs

пиле на грил *pileh na gril* — grilled chicken

пълнени пиперки *pulneni piperki* — roast peppers stuffed with mince

пържен дроб *purzhen drop* — fried liver

пържола на тиган *purzhola na tigan* — fried pork chop

сарми *sarmi* — vine or cabbage leaves stuffed with mince

свинско каварма *svinsko kavarma* — diced pork stewed with onion

свинско с кисело зеле *svinsko skiselo zeleh* — pork stewed with sauerkraut

свинско филе вретено *svinsko fileh vreteno* — pork fillet rolled with ham, cheese, and mushrooms

сирене по тракийски *sireneh po trakeeski* — feta cheese and *lookanka* baked in an earthenware pot

телешко филе с гъби *teleshko fileh zgubi* — tenderloin of veal with mushrooms

телешки гулаш *teleshki goolash* — beef goulash
филе с гъби *fileh zgubi* — pork fillet with mushrooms
шишчета *shishcheta* — lamb or pork shish kabobs
шницел *shnitsel* — breaded fried pork and beef burger
шницел натурален *shnitsel natooralen* — breaded cutlet or burger

FISH

акула *akoola* — shark
аншуа *anshwa* — anchovy fillets
бяла риба *byala riba* — pikeperch
есетра *esetra* — sturgeon
калкан *kalkan* — turbot
калмари *kalmari* — squid
кефал *kefal* — grey mullet
костур *kostoor* — perch
мерлуза *merlooza* — hake
миди *midi* — mussels
паламуд *palamoot* — tuna
попче *popcheh* — bullhead (similar to white fish)
пъстърва *pusturva* — trout
рак *rak* — crab, lobster
скариди *skaridi* — shrimps
скумрия *skoomriya* — mackerel
сом *som* — sheatfish (type of catfish)
хамсия *hamsi-ya* — sprat
цаца *tsatsa* — whitebait
чирози *chirozi* — dried salted fish
шаран *sharan* — carp
щука *shtooka* — pike

FISH DISHES

варени раци *vareni ratsi* — boiled freshwater lobsters
варена риба *varena riba* — boiled or poached fish
задушена риба *zadooshena riba* — fish stewed with local herbs and spices
маринована риба *marinovana riba* — fish pickled in marinade and spices

миди с ориз *midi soris*

паламуд *palamoot*

пълнена риба *pulnena riba*

пържена риба *purzhena riba*

риба на керемида *riba na keremida*

риба на скара *riba na skara*

риба на фурна *riba na foorna*

риба плакия *riba plakiya*

рибена чорба *ribena chorba*

салата от чирози *salata ot chirozi*

хайвер *Hiver*

boiled mussels stewed with rice

steaks of dry-cured tuna

roast fish (usually carp) filled with nut stuffing

fried fish (usually small fish)

fish roasted in a ceramic dish shaped like a roof tile

grilled fish (usually fillets of the larger varieties of fish)

oven-baked whole fish

fish stewed with mixed vegetables

clear soup of small fish and vegetables

sun-dried fillets of fish in dill and vinegar

taramasalata, caviar, fish eggs

Vegetarian Dishes

вегетариански гювеч *vegetarianski gyoovech*

имам баялдъ *imam bayalduh*

картофи огретен *kartofi ogreten*

манастирски гювеч *manastirski gyoovech*

омлет с пресен лук *omlet spresen look*

сирене на фурна *sireneh na foorna*

сирене по шопски *sireneh po shopski*

спанак със сирене *spanak sus sireneh*

тиквички пълнени със сирене *tikvichki pulneni sus sireneh*

чушки със сирене *chooshki sus sireneh*

vegetable stew with cheese

eggplant, onion, and tomato stew

potatoes baked with eggs and cheese

mixed vegetable bake

baked eggs with spring onions and cheese

feta cheese with paprika toasted in greaseproof paper

feta cheese, tomato, and egg, baked in an earthenware pot

spinach stewed with eggs and cheese

baked zucchinis stuffed with feta cheese

baked peppers stuffed with eggs and cheese

BREAD AND PASTRIES

баница *banitsa*	cheese and egg pastry
баница със спанак *banitsa sus spanak*	cheese, egg, and spinach pastry
геврек *gevrek*	bagel
кифла *kifla*	sweet bread roll filled with marmalade
мекици *mekitsi*	deep-fried light dough sprinkled with powdered sugar
милинки *milinki*	cheese buns
поничка *ponichka*	doughnut
сиренка *sirenka*	bread roll with cheese
тиквеник *tikvenik*	pumpkin pie
хляб *Hlyap*	bread

DESSERTS

ашуре *ashoorgh*	boiled whole wheat with sugar and nuts
баклава *baklava*	baklava—flaky pastry with chopped nuts, soaked in syrup
грис-халва *gris halva*	moist semolina cake
еклер *ekler*	éclair
кадаиф *kadaif*	shredded pastry soaked in syrup
кисело мляко *kiselo mlyako*	yogurt
компот *kompot*	preserved fruit in syrup
крем *krem*	custard-style pudding
крем ванилия *krem vaniliya*	vanilla custard
крем карамел *krem karamel*	crème caramel
крем шоколадов *krem shokoladof*	chocolate pudding
курабии *koorabee*	soft cookies
локум *lokoom*	Turkish delight
локум "Роза" *lokoom roza*	Turkish delight with attar of roses
локум с орехи *lokoom soreнi*	Turkish delight with walnuts
малеби *malebi*	pudding flavored with attar of roses and topped with syrup
мелба *melba*	ice cream topped with cookies, jam, and nuts
мляко с ориз *mlyako soris*	rice pudding
палачинка *palachinka*	pancake

палачинка с мед и орехи *palachinka smet i-orehi*	pancake filled with honey and crushed walnuts
палачинка с конфитюр *palachinka skonfityoor*	pancake filled with jam
паста *pasta*	cake filled with butter cream
печена тиква *pechena tikva*	baked pumpkin
саварина *savarina*	rum baba
сладко *slatko*	jam
сладолед *sladolet*	ice cream
сладолед "Ескимо" *sladolet eskimo*	ice cream on a stick, covered in chocolate
сладолед млечен *sladolet mlechen*	low-fat milk ice cream
сладолед плодов *sladolet plodof*	iced fruit juice
сладолед сметанов *sladolet smetanof*	vanilla ice cream
сладолед шоколадов *sladolet shokoladof*	chocolate ice cream
сметана *smetana*	cream
сметана разбита *smetana razbita*	whipped cream
торта *torta*	cream cake with syrup
торта "Гараш" *torta garash*	chocolate cake
торта плодова *torta plodova*	cream cake with fresh fruit
тригуна *trigoona*	baklava with whipped cream
халва *halva*	halva—sweet made from sesame seed paste and syrup
целувки *tseloofki*	meringue

FRUITS, NUTS AND SEEDS

ананас *ananas*	pineapple
бадеми *bademi*	almonds
банани *banani*	bananas
вишни *vishni*	morello cherries
грозде *grozdeh*	grapes
диня *dinya*	watermelon
кайсии *kisee*	apricots
кашу *kashoo*	cashew
киви *kivi*	kiwi
круши *krooshi*	pears
лимон *limon*	lemon
малини *malini*	raspberries

мандарини *mandarini*	tangerines
орехи *orehi*	walnuts
портокали *portokali*	oranges
праскови *praskovi*	peaches
пъпеш *pupesh*	melon
семки *semki*	sunflower seeds
сливи *slivi*	plums
смокини *smokini*	figs
фъстъци *fustutsi*	peanuts
череши *chereshi*	cherries
ябълки *yabulki*	apples
ягоди *yagodi*	strawberries

Vegetables

боб *bop*	beans
грах *grah*	peas
гъби *gubi*	mushrooms
домати *domati*	tomatoes
зеле *zeleh*	cabbage
картофи *kartofi*	potatoes
карфиол *karfiol*	cauliflower
копър *kopur*	dill
краставица *krastavitsa*	cucumber
леща *leshta*	lentils
лук *look*	onion
магданоз *magdanos*	parsley
маруля *maroolya*	lettuce
моркови *morkovi*	carrots
ориз *oris*	rice
патладжан *patlajan*	eggplant
пържени картофи *purzheni kartofi*	french fries
спанак *spanak*	spinach
тиквички *tikvichki*	zucchinis, marrows
царевица *tsarevitsa*	corn
чесън *chesun*	garlic
чушки *chooshki*	peppers

MISCELLANEOUS

варено *vareno*	boiled
горчица *gorchitsa*	mustard
задушено *zadoosheno*	braised
захар *zahar*	sugar
захарин *zaharin*	sweetener
кетчуп *ketchoop*	tomato ketchup
конфитюр *konfityoor*	jam
майонеза *mayoneza*	mayonnaise
маргарин *margarin*	margarine
масло *maslo*	butter
мед *met*	honey
на скара *naskara*	grilled
олио *olio*	vegetable oil
оцет *otset*	vinegar
печено *pecheno*	roast
пушено *poosheno*	smoked
пълнено *pulneno*	stuffed
пържено *purzheno*	fried
салам *salam*	sausage or salami
сметана *smetana*	cream
сол *sol*	salt
сурово *soorovo*	raw
сушено *soosheno*	dried
чеверме *chevermeh*	barbecued on a spit
черен пипер *cheren piper*	black pepper
яйце *yıtseh*	egg

SOFT DRINKS

айрян *iryan*	cold, diluted yogurt drink
боза *boza*	very thick sweet drink made of barley and malt
вода *voda*	water
газирана вода *gazirana voda*	soda water
кафе *kafeh*	coffee
кафе еспресо *kafeh espreso*	espresso coffee
кафе капучино *kafeh kapoochino*	cappuccino
кафе с мляко *kafeh smlyako*	coffee with milk
кафе със сметана *kafeh sus smetana*	coffee with cream

кафе нес *kafeh nes*	instant coffee
лимонада *limonada*	lemonade
минерална вода *mineralna voda*	mineral water (still)
мляко *mlyako*	milk
нектар *nektar*	juice with fruit pulp
нектар от кайсии *nektar ot kisee*	apricot nectar
нектар от праскови *nektar ot praskovi*	peach nectar
сок *sok*	fruit or fruit-flavored juice
сок от ананас *sok ot ananas*	pineapple juice
сок от вишни *sok ot vishni*	morello cherry juice
сок от домати *sok ot domati*	tomato juice
сок от малини *sok ot malini*	raspberry juice
сок от портокали *sok ot portokali*	orange juice
сок от ябълки *sok ot yabulki*	apple juice
сок от ягоди *sok ot yagodi*	strawberry juice
тоник *tonik*	tonic
турско кафе *toorsko kafeh*	Turkish-style coffee (finely ground coffee boiled in a small pot and served unfiltered)
чай *chi*	tea
чай английски *chi angleeski*	English-style tea
чай билков *chi bilkof*	mixed herbal tea
чай китайски *chi kitiski*	China tea (black or green)
чай липов *chi lipof*	lime flower tea
чай ментов *chi mentof*	peppermint tea
чай шипков *chi shipkof*	rosehip tea
топъл шоколад *topul shokolat*	hot chocolate

ALCOHOLIC DRINKS

бира *bira*	beer
бира "Алмус" *bira almus*	a brand of luxury strong lager
бира "Каменича" *bira kamenitsa*	a brand of luxury strong lager
бира "Астика" *bira astika*	a brand of luxury strong lager
бира "Галатея" *bira galateh-ya*	a brand of luxury strong lager
бира "Загорка" *bira zagorka*	a brand of luxury strong lager
бира наливна *bira nalivna*	draft beer
бира "Ломско пиво" *bira lomsko pivo*	a brand of luxury strong lager
бира "Светло пиво" *bira svetlo pivo*	lager
бира "Шуменско пиво" *bira shoomensko pivo*	a brand of luxury strong lager

MENU GUIDE

вермут *verm<u>oo</u>t* — vermouth
вино *v<u>i</u>no* — wine
водка *v<u>o</u>tka* — vodka
джин *jin* — gin
коняк *kon<u>ya</u>k* — any good quality brandy
ликьор *liky<u>o</u>r* — liqueur
мастика *mast<u>i</u>ka* — Bulgarian version of Greek ouzo
ракия *rak<u>i</u>ya* — Bulgarian traditional plum or grape brandy

шампанско *shamp<u>a</u>nsko* — champagne or any sparkling wine
уиски *w<u>i</u>ski* — whiskey

DRINKS RELATED TERMS

бяло *by<u>a</u>lo* — white
газирано *gaz<u>i</u>rano* — sparkling, carbonated
десертно вино *des<u>e</u>rtno v<u>i</u>no* — sweet wine
коктейл *kokt<u>a</u>yl* — cocktail
нискоалкохолно *n<u>i</u>skoalkoh<u>o</u>lno* — low-alcohol
полусухо *pol<u>oo</u>s<u>oo</u>ho* — medium-dry
розе *roz<u>e</u>* — pink
сухо *s<u>oo</u>ho* — dry
червено *cherv<u>e</u>no* — red

BULGARIAN WINES

Red

Гъмза *g<u>u</u>mza* — heavy, mellow, full-bodied
Каберне *kabern<u>e</u>* — full-bodied
Мавруд *mavr<u>oo</u>t* — rich, dark, heavy, dry
Мелник *m<u>e</u>lnik* — very thick, heavy, mellow, full-bodied

Мерло *merl<u>o</u>* — with a hint of strawberry
Мускател *mooskat<u>e</u>l* — sweet dessert wine
Памид *pam<u>i</u>t* — sweet, verging on rosé
Пирин *p<u>i</u>rin* — blend of *pam<u>i</u>t* and *m<u>e</u>lnik*
Тракия *tr<u>a</u>kiya* — blend of *pam<u>i</u>t* and *mavr<u>oo</u>t*

White

Димят *dimyat*	fine bouquet, very dry
Евксиноград *efksinograt*	by far the finest, dry and medium-dry varieties, rich bouquet
Карловски мискет *karlofski misket*	medium-dry, aromatic
Магарешко мляко *magareshko mlyako*	medium-dry, light
Тамянка *tamyanka*	medium-dry, light, aromatic

Sparkling

Искра *iskra*	both red and white available, medium-dry to sweet

MENU TERMS

българска национална кухня *bulgarska natsionalna koohnya*	Bulgarian national cuisine
готвач *gotvach*	cook
десерт *desert*	dessert
майстор-готвач *mistor gotvach*	chef
меню *menyoo*	menu
ордьовър *ordyovur*	hors d'oeuvre
основно ястие *osnovno yastieh*	main course
половин порция *polovin portsiya*	half (child's) portion
порция *portsiya*	portion
сметка *smetka*	check
специалитет *spetsialitet*	specialty dish

STORES AND SERVICES

Stores in Bulgaria are usually open Monday to Friday between 8 AM and 5 PM, and on Saturdays between 9 AM and 2 PM. It is quite common to find that there is a statutory siesta time in quieter places, in which case the opening times will be 8 AM–12 PM and 3–7 PM. Supermarkets and department stores usually stay open until 8 PM, including Saturdays. In the larger cities there are food stores that are open around the clock.

Goods worth looking for include replicas of antique jewelery, leather accessories, woodcarvings, embroidery, metalwork, and folk-music instruments—notably Bulgarian bagpipes **гайда** (*gida*). The best samples of these are to be found in the specialized craft museums and ethnographical centers like Etura, near the town of Gabrovo, and in the stores of the Union of Bulgarian Artists, **Съюз на българските художници** (*suyoos na bulgarskiteh hoodozhnitsi*), and the Union of Bulgarian Traditional Craftsmen, **Задруга на майсторите на художествени занаяти** (*zadrooga na mistoriteh na hoodozhestveni zanayati*). Good-quality copies of old Orthodox icons are on sale in art stores but can occasionally be bought at reasonable prices from street artists.

Other specifically Bulgarian items are yogurt **кисело мляко** (*kiselo mlyako*) and rose-petal jam **сладко от рози** (*slatko ot rozi*). Bulgaria prides itself as the home of yogurt, and it is certainly the place where the bacteria *lactobacillus bulgaricus* (that makes the milk "curdle" into yogurt) grows best, as its name confirms.

Since the advent of AIDS, shaving has been withdrawn from the range of services offered by men's hair salons. Most women's hair salons have a beauty parlor on their premises.

USEFUL WORDS AND PHRASES

bakery	фурна	*foorna*
bookstore	книжарница	*knizharnitsa*
butcher's	месарница	*mesarnitsa*

buy *(verb)*	купувам	*koopoovam*
cash register	каса	*kasa*
confectioner's	магазин за захарни изделия	*magazin za zaharni izdeliya*
department store	универсален магазин	*ooniversalen magazin*
dry cleaner's	химическо чистене	*Himichesko chisteneh*
electrical goods	електрически уреди	*elektricheski ooredi*
fish market	рибарски магазин	*ribarski magazin*
florist's	цветарски магазин	*tsvetarski magazin*
grocery	хранителни стоки	*Hranitelni stoki*
hair salon		
(*men's*)	бръснарски салон	*brusnarski salon*
(*women's*)	фризьорски салон	*frizyorski salon*
handicrafts store	магазин за народни занаяти	*magazin za narodni zanayati*
inexpensive	евтин	*eftin*
jeweler's	бижутерия	*buzhooteriya*
market	пазар	*pazar*
menswear	мъжка конфекция	*mushka konfektsiya*
newsstand	РЕП	*rep*
pastry shop	сладкарница	*slatkarnitsa*
pharmacy	аптека	*apteka*
receipt	Касова бележка	*kasova beleshka*
record store	музикален магазин	*moozikalen magazin*
sale	разпродажба	*rasprodazhba*
sales assistant		
(*man*)	продавач	*prodavach*
(*woman*)	продавачка	*prodavachka*
shoe repairer's	обущар	*obooshtar*
shoe store	магазин за обувки	*magazin za oboofki*
special offer	намалена цена	*namalena tsena*
spend	харча	*harcha*
stationery store	канцеларски пособия	*kantselarski posobiya*

STORES AND SERVICES

store	магазин	*magazin*
tailor	шивач	*shivach*
tobacco shop	магазин за цигари	*magazin za tsigari*
toy store	магазин за играчки	*magazin za igrachki*
travel agent	туристическо бюро	*tooristichesko byooro*
women's wear	дамска конфекция	*damska konfektsiya*

Excuse me, where is/are …?
Извинете, къде се намира/намират …?
izvineteh, kudeh seh namira/namirat

Where is there a … store?
Къде има магазин за …?
kudeh ima magazin za

Where is the … department?
Къде е отделът за …?
kudeh eh otdela za

Is there an outdoor market here?
Има ли пазар тук?
ima li pazar took

When does the market open?
Кога се отваря пазарът?
koga seh otvarya pazara

I'd like …
Дайте ми …
diteh mi …

Do you have …?
Имате ли …
imateh li

How much is this?
Колко струва това?
kolko stroova tova

Where do I pay?
Къде да платя?
kudeh da platya

Do you take credit cards?
Приемате ли кредитни карти?
pri-emateh li kreditni karti

I think perhaps you've shortchanged me
Струва ми се, че има грешка в рестото
stroova mi seh, cheh ima greshka frestoto

May I have a receipt?
Бихте ли ми дали касова бележка?
bihteh li mi dali kasova beleshka

May I have a bag, please?
Бихте ли ми дали торбичка, моля?
bihteh li mi dali torbichka, molya

I'm just looking
Само разглеждам
samo razglezhdam

I'll come back later
Ще дойда пак по-късно
shteh doyda pak po kusno

Do you have any more …?
Имате ли още от ...?
imateh li oshteh ot

Do you have anything less expensive?
Имате ли нещо по-евтино?
imateh li neshto po eftino

Do you have anything larger/smaller?
Имате ли по-голям/по-малък размер?
imateh li po golyam/po maluk razmer

May I try it on?
Може ли да го пробвам?
mozheh li da go probvam

Does it come in other colors?
Имате ли от това в други цветове?
imateh li ottova vdroogi tsvetoveh

Could you wrap it for me?
Бихте ли го опаковали, моля?
bihteh li go opakovali, molya

I'd like to change this, please
Бихте ли ми сменили това, моля?
bihteh li mi smenili tova, molya

I don't have the receipt
Нямам касова бележка
nyamam kasova beleshka

Can I have a refund?
Мога ли да го върна?
moga li da go vurna

What is the price per kilo?
Каква е цената за килограм?
kakva eh tsenata za kilogram

Could you write that down?
Бихте ли ми написали това?
bihteh li mi napisali tova

I'll have a piece of that cheese
Дайте ми парче от това сирене
diteh mi parcheh ottova sireneh

About 250/500 grams
Около двеста и педесет/петстотин грама
okolo dvesta i pedeset/petstotin grama

A kilo/half a kilo of …, please
Килограм/половин килограм от ..., моля
kvilogram/polovin kilogram ot …, molya

Can you mend this?
Можете ли да поправите това?
mozheteh li da popraviteh tova

I'd like this skirt/these pants dry-cleaned
Искам да оставя тази пола/тези панталони за химическо
  чистене
iskam da ostavya tazi pola/tezi pantaloni za himichesko chisteneh

When will it/they be ready?
Кога ще бъде готова/бъдат готови?
koga shteh budeh gotova/budat gotovi

I'd like to make an appointment
Искам да запазя час
iskam da zapazya chas

I want a cut and blow-dry
Подстригване и изсушаване, моля
potstrigvaneh i isooshavaneh, molya

Just a trim, please
Скъсете я съвсем малко, моля
skuseteh ya sufsem malko, molya

A bit more off here, please
Скъсете я още малко тук, моля
skuseteh ya oshteh malko took, molya

Not too much off!
Не я скъсявайте много!
neh ya skusyaviteh mnogo

I don't want any hairspray
Не слагайте лак, моля
neh slagiteh lak, molya

THINGS YOU'LL HEAR

kakvo shteh zhelaeteh?
What would you like?

kazheteh, molya
May I help you?

suzhalyavam, no tova go svurshiнmeh
I'm sorry, this item is no longer in stock

tova eh fsichko, koeto mozhem da vi predlozhim
This is all we have

sheh vi opsloozha slet minoota
I'll be with you in a moment

molya neh pipiteh
Please don't touch

tova li eh fsichko?
Is that all?

shteh zhelaeteh li neshto droogo?
Do you want something else?

imateh li drebni?
Have you got any small change?

eto restoto
Here's the change

kak ya iskateh?
How would you like it?

dostatuchno li ya skusiн?
Is that short enough?

da vi slozha li lak za kosa?
Would you like hairspray?

da vi slozha li balsam?
Would you like any conditioner?

THINGS YOU'LL SEE

антикварен магазин	*antikvaren magazin*	antiques shop
антикварна книжарница	*antikvarna knizharitsa*	secondhand bookstore
аптека	*apteka*	pharmacy
асансьор	*asansyor*	elevator
бельо	*belyo*	lingerie, underwear
бижутерия	*bizhooteriya*	jeweler's
бирария	*birariya*	beer and grills joint, bar
бои и железария	*bwi i zhelezariya*	DIY
бръснарски салон	*brusnarski salon*	barber's shop, men's hair salon
вещи под наем	*veshti pod naem*	items for rent
вино	*vino*	wines
висококачествен	*visokokachestven*	high quality
галантерия	*galanteriya*	haberdashery, hosiery
деликатеси	*delikatesi*	delicatessen
домашни потреби	*domashni potrebi*	household goods
евтино	*eftino*	inexpensive
електроуреди	*elektro-ooredi*	electrical goods
етаж	*etash*	floor
задруга на майсторите на художествени занаяти	*zadrooga na mistoriteh na hoodozhestveni zanayati*	the Union of Bulgarian Traditional Craftsmen
затворено	*zatvoreno*	closed
захарни изделия	*zaharni izdeliya*	confectionery
играчки	*igrachki*	toys
измиване	*izmivaneh*	wash
каса	*kasa*	pay here
кафе	*kafeh*	coffee shop
килими	*kilimi*	carpets

→

75

кожени изделия	kozheni izdeliya	leather goods
книжарница	knizharnitsa	bookstore
конфекция	konfektsiya	ready-to-wear clothes
луксозен	looksozen	luxury
магазин бебе	magazin bebeh	baby clothes
месни изделия	mesni izdeliya	sausage meats
месо	meso	meat
млечни продукти	mlechni prodookti	dairy products
мода	moda	fashion
моля вземете кошница	molya vzemeteh koshnitsa	please take a basket
моля не пипайте	molya neh pipiteh	please don't touch
намалени цени	namaleni tseni	reductions
народни занаяти	narodni zanayati	handicrafts
облекло	obleklo	clothing
обувки	oboofki	footwear
отворено	otvoreno	open
отдел	otdel	department
пазар	pazar	market
партер	parter	first floor
парфюмерия	parfyoomeriya	perfumery
пасмантерия	pasmanteriya	haberdashery
платове	platoveh	fabrics
плодове и зеленчуци	plodoveh i zelenchootsi	fruits and vegetables
поправка на обувки	poprafka na oboofki	shoe repairs
подстригваме	podstrigvaneh	haircut
пресен	presen	fresh
приемаме стока	priemameh stoka	(closed for) taking deliveries
разпродажба	rasprodazhba	sale
ревизия	reviziya	(closed for) inventory
РЕП	rep	newsstand

→

76

самообслужване	*samo-opsloozhivaneh*	self-service
сирене	*sireneh*	cheese
Съюз на българските художници	*suyoos na bulgarskiteh hoodozhnitsi*	Union of Bulgarian Artists
спиртни напитки	*spirtni napitki*	alcoholic drinks
спортен магазин	*sporten magazin*	sports goods
сутерен	*sooteren*	basement
трикотаж	*trikotash*	knitwear
туристическо бюро	*tooristichesko byooro*	travel agent's
универсален магазин	*ooniversalen magazin*	department store
фризьорски салон	*frizyorski salon*	women's hairstylist
химическо чистене	*Himichesko chisteneh*	dry cleaner's
хляб	*Hlyap*	bread
хранителни стоки	*Hranitelni stoki*	grocer's
цветя	*tsvetya*	flowers
цена	*tsena*	price
цигари	*tsigari*	tobacco shop

SPORTS

Under communism, nearly all sports facilities in Bulgaria were intended to serve only professional sportsmen and sportswomen. Jogging, and sometimes swimming, were the only sports that ordinary members of the public could practice.

There are now a few Western-style leisure centers in the larger cities, offering aerobics classes and well-equipped gyms, saunas, etc. Swimming pools can be found in most larger cities; they are clean but can be overcrowded. Tennis courts are similarly confined to the cities, usually in parks, and are very busy. Both swimming and tennis, as well as miniature golf (but not ordinary golf), are more readily available at coastal resorts. Renting a bicycle is also possible at most of the coastal resorts. Facilities for all water sports are available there, too, with the possible exception of scuba diving. A flag warning system operates on most beaches: black means that swimming is temporarily suspended on safety grounds; red is for dangerous conditions; and white means all-clear.

Mountaineering and hiking are quite popular and attract an increasing number of visitors to the country.

Skiing is the most popular winter sport. The two purpose-built ski resorts, Borovets and Pamporovo, have all the usual facilities (ski tows, chairlifts, equipment rental, etc.) at reasonable prices. Skiing in Vitosha is also good and has the added attraction of the capital, Sofia, being only 20 minutes' drive from the hotel area. If package-vacation skiing does not appeal to you, try Bansko and Malyovitsa in the southwest of the country.

Special permits are required for fishing and hunting, but "safari"-type tours can be organized through travel agencies.

USEFUL WORDS AND PHRASES

athletics	атлетика	*atletika*
badminton	бадминтон	*badminton*
ball	топка	*topka*
basketball	баскетбол	*basketbol*

beach	плаж	*plash*
bicycle	велосипед	*velosipet*
bowling	боулинг	*bowlink*
chairlift	открит лифт	*otkrit lift*
fishing	риболов	*ribolof*
fishing rod	въдица	*vuditsa*
goggles	очила за плуване	*ochila za ploovaneh*
gymnastics	гимнастика	*gimnastika*
hunting	лов	*lof*
mountaineering	алпинизъм	*alpinizum*
parascending	парашут	*parashoot*
pedal boat	водно колело	*vodno kolelo*
piste	писта	*pista*
racket	ракета	*raketa*
riding	езда	*ezda*
rowboat	гребна лодка	*grebna lotka*
run (*verb*)	бягам	*byagam*
sailboard	платноходка	*platnohotka*
sailing	ветроходство	*vetrohotstvo*
skate (*verb*)	карам кънки	*karam kunki*
skates	кънки	*kunki*
ski bindings	ски автомати	*ski aftomati*
ski boots	ски обувки	*ski oboofki*
ski lift	ски лифт	*ski lift*
ski pass	карта за ски лифт	*karta za ski lift*
skis	ски	*ski*
ski tow	ски влек	*ski vlek*
sledge	шейна	*shayna*
snorkel	шнорхел	*shnorhel*
soccer	футбол	*footbol*
soccer match	футболен мач	*footbolen match*
stadium	стадион	*stadi-on*
swim (*verb*)	плувам	*ploovam*
swimming pool	плувен басейн	*plooven basayn*
tennis	тенис	*tenis*
tennis court	тенис корт	*tenis kort*
volleyball	волейбол	*volaybol*

walking	ходене	_hodeneh_
water-skiing	каране на водни ски	_karaneh na vodni ski_
water skis	водни ски	_vodni ski_
wet suit	водолазен костюм	_vodolazen kostyoom_
yacht	яхта	_yahta_

Where can I rent …?
Къде мога да наема ...?
kadeh moga da naema

How do I get to the beach?
Как да отида до плажа?
kak da otida do plazha

How deep is the water here?
Колко е дълбока водата тук?
kolko eh dulboka vodata took

Is there an indoor/outdoor pool here?
Тук има ли закрит/открит басейн?
took ima li zakrit/otkrit basayn

Is it safe to swim here?
Безопасно ли е да се плува тук?
bezopasno li eh da seh ploova took

Can I fish here?
Тук може ли да се лови риба?
took mozheh li da seh lovi riba

Do I need a license?
Нужно ли е разрешително?
noozhno li eh razreshitelno

I would like to rent a beach umbrella
Искам да наема чадър
iskam da naema chadur

How much does it cost per hour/day?
Колко струва на час/на ден?
kolko stroova na chas/na den

I would like to take water-skiing lessons
Искам да вземам уроци по водни ски
iskam da vzema oorotsi povodni ski

Where can I buy skiing equipment?
Къде мога да купя ски оборудване?
kudeh moga da koopya ski oboroodvaneh

There's something wrong with this binding
Този автомат не работи
tozi aftomat neh raboti

I'd like to try cross-country skiing *(said by a man/woman)*
Бих искал/искала да опитам ски крос
bih iskal/iskala da opitam ski kros

How much is a daily/weekly pass for the ski lift?
Колко струва еднодневна/седмична карта за ски лифта?
kolko stroova ednodnevna/sedmichna karta za ski lifta

Can you recommend a good place to ski?
Бихте ли ми препоръчали подходяша местност за ски?
bihteh li mi preporuchali pothodyashta mesnost za ski

Where are the beginners' slopes?
Къде е пистата за начинаещи?
kudeh eh pistata za nachinaeshti

Things You'll See

алея за велосипеди	*alehya za velosipedi*	bicycle path
билети	*bileti*	tickets
велосипеди	*velosipedi*	bicycles
влизането забранено	*vlizaneto zabraneno*	restricted area
водни спортове	*vodni sportoveh*	water sports
душове	*dooshoveh*	showers

→

81

закрит плувен басейн	zakrit plooven basayn	indoor swimming pool
играта с топки забранена	igrata stopki zabranena	no ball games
кални бани	kalni bani	mud baths
къпането забранено	kupaneto zabraneno	bathing prohibited
лифт	lift	cable car, chairlift
ловенето на риба забранено	loveneto na riba zabraneno	no fishing
нудистки плаж	noodiski plash	nudist beach
опасно за живота	opasno za zhivota	danger high voltage
опасност от лавини	opasnost ot lavini	danger of avalanche
открит плувен басейн	otkrit plooven basayn	outdoor swimming pool
плаж	plash	beach
плуването забранено	ploovaneto zabreneno	no swimming
скачането забранено	skachaneto zabraneno	no diving
спортен център	sporten tsentur	sports center
под наем	pod naem	for rent
платноходки	platnohotki	sailboats
пристанищна охрана	pristanishtna ohrana	harbor police
ски влек	ski vlek	ski tow
ски писта	ski pista	ski piste
съблекални жени	sublekalni zheni	women's changing rooms
съблекални мъже	sublekalni muzheh	men's changing rooms
уроци по водни ски	oorotsi po vodni ski	water-skiing lessons
яхт-клуб	yaнt kloop	marina

POST OFFICES AND BANKS

Post offices in Bulgaria can be recognized by a yellow sign. Most mailboxes are yellow and so is the sign for telephones. Sending your mail from the central post office in a town will save you up to a day in delivery time; letters sent by "express" mail may not be delivered faster and may well be slower than ordinary mail. Anything more than a postcard is worth sending by registered mail **препоръчано писмо** (*preporuchano pismo*) if you want to be sure that it will leave the country intact; this is generally not as expensive as it is in the West. Allow well over a week for a letter or a postcard to arrive at any address in the US. Packages for abroad have to be taken unwrapped to the post office and wrapped at the counter to allow for examination by a customs official.

Post offices in smaller towns are open from 8:30 AM to 5:30 PM and in cities from 8 AM to 6 PM Mondays to Saturdays.

The official exchange rate of the major foreign currencies, announced daily by the National Bank, is an advisory one; tourist exchange rates are usually just under this figure. There is no shortage of exchange offices, **бюро за обмяна** (*byooro za obmyana*), but it will not be necessary or advisable to change more than you will need for the day. Most stores and hotels will not accept checks or credit cards. ATMs can now be found in the major banks in major cities and towns, and can be used reliably. Since there is hardly an alternative to paying by cash in Bulgaria, carrying your money around with you seems inevitable (see also Hotels, p. 19).

Changing money with street dealers is still an offense under Bulgarian law and, although this law is less strictly enforced since the demise of communism, this activity has lost much of its previous attraction since few of the dealers can match or improve on the official exchange rate, while the possibility of being cheated still remains high. In theory, you are also still required to keep all exchange receipts and be able to produce them on demand when you leave the country.

In July 1999, new bills and coins were introduced at the rate of
1 new lev = 1000 old lev. By December 1999, all old bills and
coins will have been superseded. The value of the lev has been
pegged to the German Deutschmark since 1997.
1 DM = 1 new lev.

USEFUL WORDS AND PHRASES

airmail	въздушна поща	vuzdooshna poshta
bank	банка	banka
bill (banknote)	банкнота	banknota
cash	пари	pari
change (verb)	обменям	obmenyam
check	чек	chek
counter	гише	gisheh
credit card	кредитна карта	kreditna karta
customs form	митническа	mitnicheska
	декларация	deklaratsiya
delivery	разнасяне	raznasyaneh
dollar	долар	dolar
envelopes	пликове	plikoveh
exchange rate	обменен курс	obmenen koors
form	бланка	blanka
general delivery	до поискване	do poiskvaneh
international	международен	mezhdoonaroden
money order	пощенски превод	poshtenski prevot
letter	писмо	pismo
letter carrier	пощаджия	poshtadziya
mail (noun)	поща	poshta
mailbox	пощенска кутия	poshtenska kootiya
money order	запис	zapis
package/parcel	колет	kolet
postage rates	пощенска тарифа	poshtenska tarifa
postal order	пощенски запис	poshtenski zapis
postcard	картичка	kartichka
post office	поща	poshta

registered letter	препоръчано писмо	*preporuchano pismo*
stamp	марка	*marka*
surface mail	обикновена поща	*obiknovena poshta*
traveler's check	пътнически чек	*putnicheski chek*
writing paper	листи за писма	*listi za pisma*
zip code	пощенски код	*poshtenski kot*

How much is a letter/postcard to ...?
Колко струва писмо/картичка до ...?
kolko stroova pismo/kartichka do

I'd like four 7-leva stamps
Моля, дайте ми четири марки по седем лева
molya, diteh mi chetiri marki po sedem leva

I want to register this letter
Искам да изпратя това писмо препоръчано
iskam da ispratya tova pismo preporuchano

I want to send this parcel to ...
Искам да изпратя този колет до ...
iskam da ispratya tozi kolet do

Where can I mail this?
Къде мога да изпратя това?
kudeh moga da ispratya tova

Is there any mail for me?
Имате ли поща за мен?
imateh li poshta za men

I'd like to send a telegram
Искам да изпратя телеграма
iskam da ispratya telegrama

This is to go airmail
Въздушна поща, моля
vuzdooshna poshta, molya

I'd like to change this into leva
Искам да обменя това в левове
iskam da obmenya tova flevoveh

Can I cash these traveler's checks?
Мога ли да обменя тези пътнически чекове?
moga li da obmenya tezi putnicheski chekoveh

What is the exchange rate for the dollar?
Какъв е обменният курс на долара?
kakuf eh obmenniya koors na dolara

THINGS YOU'LL SEE

адрес	*adres*	address
банкноти	*banknoti*	bills (banknotes)
бърза поща	*burza poshta*	express
бюро	*byooro*	office
бюро за обмяна	*byooro za obmyana*	currency exchange office
валута	*valoota*	foreign currency
въздушна поща	*vuzdooshna poshta*	airmail
гише	*gisheh*	teller, counter
гише колети	*gisheh koleti*	parcels counter
директор	*direktor*	(bank) manager
долари	*dolari*	dollars
до поискване	*do poiskvaneh*	general delivery
ДСК	*de-seh-ka*	National Savings Bank
запис	*zapis*	money order
затворено	*zatvoreno*	closed
картичка	*kartichka*	postcard
каса	*kasa*	cash desk
касиер	*kasier*	cashier
квитанция	*kvitantsiya*	receipt

→

марка за страната	*marka za stranata*	inland postage
марка за чужбина	*marka za choozhbina*	postage abroad
марки	*marki*	stamps
монети	*moneti*	coins
населено място	*naseleno myasto*	place
отворено	*otvoreno*	open
пакет	*paket*	package
паричен запис	*parichen zapis*	money order
печатно	*pechatno*	printed matter
писмо	*pismo*	letter
подател	*podatel*	sender
получател	*poloochatel*	addressee
почивка	*pochifka*	back in a few minutes
поща	*poshta*	post office, mail, mailbox
пощенски код	*poshtenski kot*	zip code
преводи	*prevodi*	transfers
препоръчани писма	*preporuchani pisma*	registered mail
работно време	*rabotno vremeh*	opening hours
сметка	*smetka*	account
събира се в ...	*subira seh v ...*	collection times ...
справки	*sprafki*	information
такса	*taxa*	charge
тарифа	*tarifa*	scale of charges
телеграми	*telegrami*	telegrams
централна поща	*tsentralna poshta*	central post office
чек	*chek*	check

COMMUNICATIONS

Telephones: Public phones are easy to come by in all towns.
Some public phones take phonecards, which are available from
post offices, stores, and street kiosks in various denominations.
There are currently two types of phonecard: BETCOM (for
blue phones) and BULFON (for orange phones). The quality
of international connections is good and may be better than
the quality of local and long-distance internal calls.

Making a long-distance or international call is easy from the
telephone sections of post offices. The central ones in most
cities stay open until 11 PM, while the one in Sofia never
closes and becomes rather busy at night. You may have to wait
in line for a while until a phone booth becomes available. You
dial the number yourself and pay afterward.

Phoning abroad from hotels is possible but it is very expensive.
To call the USA and Canada, dial 001, for Australia the code is
0061, for New Zealand 0064, for the UK 0044, and for Eire
00353. To dial direct, first use the international code and then
the STD code minus the initial 0.

The tones you hear on Bulgarian phones are as follows:

Dial tone: alternate short and long tones;
Ringing: long tones separated by longer pauses;
Busy: short equal on/off tones.

USEFUL WORDS AND PHRASES

answering machine	телефонен секретар	*telefonen sekretar*
call (*noun*)	телефонен разговор	*telefonen razgovor*
call (*verb*)	обаждам се по телефона	*obazhdam seh po telefona*
code	код	*kot*
collect call	разговор "за тяхна сметка"	*razgovor za tyahna smetka*
dial (*verb*)	избирам	*izbiram*

dial tone	сигнал за избиране	signal za izbiraneh
directory assistance	справки	sprafki
email address	имейл адрес	imayl adres
extension	вътрешен номер	vutreshen nomer
international call	международен разговор	mezhdoonaroden razgovor
internet	интернет	internet
mobile phone	мобифон	mobifon
modem	модем	modem
number	номер	nomer
operator (man)	телефонист	telefonist
(woman)	телефонистка	telefoniska
payphone	телефонен автомат	telefonen aftomat
phone book	телефонен указател	telefonen ookazatel
phonecard	фонокарта	fonokarta
photocopier	ксерокс	kseroks
receiver	слушалка	slooshalka
telephone	телефон	telefon
telephone booth	телефонна кабина	telefonna kabina
(in post office)	кабина	kabina
website	уеб сайт	ooeb sayt

Where is the nearest phone booth?
Къде е най-близката телефонна кабина?
kudeh eh ni-bliskata telefonna kabina

I would like the phone book for …
Бихте ли ми дали указателя на …?
binteh li mi dali ookazatelya na

Can I call abroad from here?
Мога ли да се обадя в чужбина от тук?
moga li da seh obadya fchoozhbina ottook

How much is a call to …?
Колко струва един разговор до …?
kolko stroova edin razgovor do

COMMUNICATIONS

I would like to make a collect call
Искам да се обадя "за тяхна сметка"
iskam da seh obadya za tyahna smetka

I would like a number in … (said by a man/woman)
Бих искал/искала да се обадя до …
biн iskal/iskala da seh obadya do …

Hello, this is … speaking
Ало, обажда се …
alo, obazhda seh

Is that …?
… ли е на телефона?
… li eh na telefona

Speaking (said by a man/woman)
Той/тя е на телефона
toy/tya eh na telefona

I would like to speak to …
Мога ли да говоря …
moga li da govorya

Extension …, please
Моля вътрешен …
molya vutreshen

Please tell him/her … called
Моля, предайте му/и, че … се е обаждал/обаждала
molya, prediteh moo/i, cheh … seh eh bazhdal/obazhdala

Ask him/her to call me back, please
Моля, предайте му/и да ми се обади
molya, prediteh moo/i da mi seh obadi

My number is …
Номерът ми е …
nomera mi eh

COMMUNICATIONS

Do you know where he/she is?
Знаете ли къде е той/тя?
znaeteh li kudeh eh toy/tya

When will he/she be back?
Кога ще се върне?
kvoga shteh seh vurneh

Could you leave him/her a message?
Бихте ли му/и предали?
bihteh li moo/i predali

I'll call back later
Ще позвъня по-късно
shteh pozvunya po-kusno

Sorry, I have the wrong number
Грешка, извинете
greshka, izvineteh

Sorry, you have the wrong number
Имате грешка
imateh greshka

What's your fax number/email address?
Какъв е вашият факс/имейл адрес?
kakuv e vashiya faks/imayl adres

Did you get my fax/email?
Получихте ли моя факс/имейл?
poloochihteh li moya faks/imayl

Please resend your fax
Моля изпратете факса отново
molya izprateteh faksa otnovo

Can I send a email/fax from here?
Мога ли да изпратя имейл/факс от тук?
moga li da izpratya imayl/faks ot tuk

THINGS YOU'LL HEAR

skogo iskateh da govoriteh?
Whom would you like to speak to?

imateh greshka
You've got the wrong number

koy eh na telefona?
Who's speaking?

koy eh vashiya nomer?
What is your number?

suzhalyavam, no nego go/naya ya nyama
Sorry, he/she is not in

toy/tya shteh seh vurneh fshes chasa
He/she will be back at six o'clock

obadeteh seh ootreh, ako obichateh
Please call again tomorrow

shteh moo/i predam, cheh steh seh obazhdali
I'll tell him/her you called

THINGS YOU'LL SEE

автоматично избиране	*aftomatichno izbiraneh*	direct dialing
градски разговор	*gratski razgovor*	local call
междуградски разговор	*mezhdoogratski razgovor*	long-distance call
не работи	*neh raboti*	out of order
повреди	*povredi*	faults service
тарифа	*tarifa*	charges
телефонна палата	*telefonna palata*	telephone section

EMERGENCIES

Information on local health services can be obtained from
tourist information offices. In an emergency, dial 150 for an
ambulance, 160 for the fire department, and 166 for the police.
In the event of your car breaking down, phone 146 for help
from the Bulgarian Union of Motorists; 163 for breakdown
service from the nearest garage; and 162 for General Rescue
Services. If you lose your passport, you should notify the US
embassy as well as the police.

Everyone is required to carry an ID card or a passport at all
times. Drivers are obliged to have their licenses on them and
to produce them on demand to the traffic police **KAT** (*kat*).

Some hotels may keep foreigners' passports overnight at the
reception desk; this is a hangover from the cumbersome
procedure for the administration of foreign visitors from
communist times and is no cause for alarm.

If you happen to be the injured party in any kind of trouble,
you may still be detained by the police (sometimes overnight)
until the circumstances are clarified. Patience and a good
interpreter will be essential in such cases. If things get difficult,
make a point of frequently invoking the name of your embassy
—this should ease matters considerably.

USEFUL WORDS AND PHRASES

accident	злополука	*zlopolooka*
(*car*)	катастрофа	*katastrofa*
emergency room	спешни случаи	*speshni sloochayi*
ambulance	линейка	*linayka*
American	Американско	*amerikansko*
embassy	посолство	*posolstvo*
assault (*verb*)	нападам	*napadam*
breakdown	авария	*avariya*
breakdown	аварийна сервизна	*avareena servizna*
recovery	служба	*sloozhba*
break down	поврежда се	*povrezhda seh*

British embassy	Британско посолство	*britansko posolstvo*
burglar	крадец	*kradets*
burglary	кражба	*krazhba*
crash *(noun)*	сблъскване	*zbluskvaneh*
crash *(verb)*	сблъсквам се	*zbluskvam seh*
fire	пожар	*pozhar*
fire department	пожарна команда	*pozharna komanda*
flood *(noun)*	наводнение	*navodnenieh*
injured	наранен	*naranen*
lose	загубвам	*zagoobvam*
money	пари	*pari*
passport	паспорт	*pasport*
pickpocket	крадец	*kradets*
police	полиция	*politsiya*
police station	полицейски участък	*politsayski oochastuk*
rob	ограбвам	*ograbvam*
steal	крада	*krada*
theft	кражба	*krazhba*
thief	крадец	*kradets*
tow *(verb)*	тегля	*teglya*

Help!
Помощ!
pomosht

Look out!
Внимавай!
vnimavi

Stop!
Спри!
spri

This is an emergency!
Спешен случай!
speshen sloochı

Get an ambulance!
Повикайте линейка!
povikiteh linayka

Please send an ambulance to …
Моля, изпратете линейка на …
molya, isprateteh linayka na

Please come to …
Моля, елате на …
molya, elateh na

My address is …
Адресът ми е …
adresa mi eh

We've had a break-in
В стаята ни са влизали крадци
fstiata ni sa vlizali krattsi

There's a fire at …
Има пожар на …
ima pozhar na

Someone's been injured
Има наранен човек
ima naranen chovek

My passport/car has been stolen
Откраднали са ми паспорта/колата
otkradnali sa mi pasporta/kolata

The registration number is …
Регистрационният номер е …
registratsi-onni-ya nomer eh

My car's been broken into
Крадци са влезли с взлом в колата ми
krattsi sa vlezli z-vzlom fkolata mi

95

I've lost my traveler's checks
Изгубил съм си пътническите чекове
izgoobil sum si putnicheskiteh chekoveh

I want to report a stolen credit card
Искам да съобщя за открадната кредитна карта
iskam da suhopshtya za otkradnata kreditna karta

It was stolen from my room
Откраднаха го от моята стая
otkradnaнa go ot moyata stia

I lost it in/at …
Иагубих го в/на …
izgoobiн go v/na

My luggage is missing
Моят багаж го няма
moya bagash go nyama

Has my luggage turned up yet?
Намерен ли е моят багаж?
nameren li eh moya bagash

I've been mugged
Ограбиха ме на улицата
ograbiнa meh na oolitsata

My son's missing
Синът ми изчезна
sina mi ischezna

He's … years old
Той е на … години
toy eh na … godini

I've locked myself out
Заключих се вън от стаята
zaklyoochiн seh vun ot stiata

He's drowning
Той се дави
tvoy seh davi

She can't swim
Тя не може да плува
tya neh mozheh da ploova

THINGS YOU'LL SEE

болница	*bolnitsa*	hospital
бърза помощ	*burza pomosht*	ambulance
изберете ...	*isbereteh ...*	dial ...
КАТ	*kat*	traffic police
обслужва се 24 часа	*opsloozhva seh 24 chasa*	24-hour service
пожар	*pozhar*	fire
полицейски участък	*politsayski oochastuk*	police station
полиция	*politsiya*	police, police station
първа помощ	*purva pomosht*	first aid
спасител	*spasitel*	lifeguard
спешни случаи	*speshni sloochai*	emergencies
травматология	*travmatologiya*	emergency room

THINGS YOU'LL HEAR

koy eh vashi-ya adres?
What's your address?

kadeh steh?
Where are you?

mozheteh li da go opisheteh?
Can you describe it/him?

HEALTH

Pharmacies—**аптека** (*apteka*)—can give medical advice for minor ailments and first aid if necessary. Practically all medicines that are available can be bought with or without a prescription. Cosmetics, toiletries, and accessories are also sold in pharmacies. All towns have at least one pharmacy that is open all night.

For more serious illnesses, you would have to go to the nearest **поликлиника** (*poliklinika*), which is a hospital consisting of numerous general practitioners and consultants' offices—like a very large outpatient department. All **поликлиника** have facilities for performing minor surgery; most of them also have a dispensary on the premises.

In an emergency, an ambulance can be called by phoning 150. The service is free. Bulgarian ambulances tend not to be as fast or as well-equipped as their counterparts in the West but this is no fault of the hard-working staff, rather due to the fact that the former communist rulers had a special ambulance service to themselves with vehicles supplied by Mercedes, so they never felt personally compelled to improve the general service.

It will help if you could arrange for an interpreter to accompany you to the doctor, but if you cannot, don't panic—most doctors in Bulgaria speak a Western European language. Summon up all your knowledge of German (if you have any), as this is one of the most widely spoken foreign languages in Bulgaria.

It is advisable to take any medicines you need and also a high-factor sunblock because you may not be able to find what you need in Bulgarian pharmacies.

In Sofia, there is a special clinic for foreigners (which is not free of charge) and a pharmacy selling Western drugs for hard currency. Ask at the reception desk of any good hotel in the city for directions.

USEFUL WORDS AND PHRASES

accident	злополука	zlopolooka
ambulance	линейка	linayka
anemic	анемичен	anemichen
appendicitis	апендицит	apenditsit
appendix	апендикс	apendix
aspirin	аспирин	aspirin
asthma	астма	astma
backache	болки в гърба	bolki vgurba
bandage	превръзка	prevruska
(adhesive)	лейкопласт	laykoplast
bite (by dog)	ухапване	oohapvaneh
(by insect)	ужилване	oozhilvaneh
bladder	пикочен мехур	pikochen mehoor
blister	пъпка, пришка	pupka, prishka
blood	кръв	kruf
blood donor	кръводарител	kruvodaritel
burn (noun)	изгаряне	izgaryaneh
cancer	рак	rak
chest	гръден кош	gruden kosh
chicken pox	шарка, варицела	sharka, varitsela
cold (noun)	настинка	nastinka
concussion	мозъчно сътресение	mozuchno sutresenieh
constipation	запек	zapek
contact lenses	контактни лещи	kontaktni leshti
corn	мазол	mazol
cough (noun)	кашлица	kashlitsa
cut (noun)	порязване	poryazvaneh
dentist	зъболекар	zubolekar
diabetes	диабет	di-abet
diarrhea	диария	diariya
dizziness	виене на свят	vieneh na svyat
doctor	лекар	lekar
earache	болки в ухото	bolki foohoto
fever	треска	treska

filling	пломба	*plomba*
first aid	първа помощ	*purva pomosht*
flu	грип	*grip*
fracture	счупване	*shchoopvaneh*
German measles	дребна шарка, рубеола	*drebna sharka, roobehola*
glasses	очила	*ochila*
hay fever	сенна хрема	*senna hrema*
headache	главоболие	*glavobolieh*
heart	сърце	*surtseh*
heart attack	инфаркт	*infarkt*
hemorrhage	кръвоизлив	*kruvoizlif*
hepatitis	хепатит	*hepatit*
HIV positive	ХИВ-позитивен	*'HIV' pozititven*
hospital	болница	*bolnitsa*
ill	болен	*bolen*
indigestion	стомашно разстройство	*stomashno rastroystvo*
inhaler	инхалатор	*inhalator*
injection	инжекция	*inzhektsiya*
itch	сърбеж	*surbesh*
kidney	бъбрек	*bubrek*
lump	подутина, бучка	*podootina, boochka*
measles	дребна шарка, морбили	*drebna sharka, morbili*
migraine	мигрена	*migrena*
motion sickness	морска болест	*morska bolest*
mumps	заушка	*zaooshka*
nausea	повдигане	*povdiganeh*
nurse (*female*)	сестра	*sestra*
operation	операция	*operatsiya*
optician	оптик	*optik*
pain	болка	*bolka*
penicillin	пеницилин	*penitsilin*
pharmacy	аптекар	*aptekar*
plaster of Paris	гипс	*gips*
pneumonia	пневмония	*pnevmoni-ya*

pregnant	бременна	*bremenna*
prescription	рецепта	*retsepta*
rheumatism	ревматизъм	*revmatizum*
scald (*noun*)	изгаряне с вряла течност	*izgaryaneh zvryala technost*
scratch (*noun*)	одраскване	*odraskvaneh*
smallpox	едра шарка, вариола	*edra sharka, variola*
sore throat	възпалено гърло	*vuspaleno gurlo*
splinter (*noun*)	парче	*parcheh*
sprain (*noun*)	изкълчване	*iskulchvaneh*
sting (*noun*)	ужилване	*oozhilvaneh*
stomach	стомах	*stomaн*
temperature	температура	*temperatoora*
tonsils	сливици	*slivitsi*
toothache	зъбобол	*zubobol*
ulcer	язва	*yazva*
vaccination	ваксинация	*vaksinatsiya*
vomit (*verb*)	повръщам	*povrushtam*

I have a pain in …
Боли ме ...
boli meh

I do not feel well
Не се чувствам добре
neh seh choofstvam dobreh

I feel faint (*said by a man/woman*)
Чувствам се отпаднал/отпаднала
choofstvam seh otpadnal/otpadnala

I feel sick
Лошо ми е
losho mi eh

I feel dizzy
Вие ми се свят
vieh mi seh svyat

It hurts here
Боли ме тук
boli meh took

It's a sharp pain
Болката е остра
bolkata eh ostra

It's a dull pain
Болката е тъпа
bolkata eh tupa

It hurts all the time
Боли ме непрекъснато
boli meh neprekusnato

It only hurts now and then
Боли ме от време на време
boli meh ot vremeh na vremeh

It hurts when you touch it
Боли ме при допир
boli me pri dopir

It stings
Щипе
shtipeh

It aches
Боли ме
boli meh

I have a temperature
Имам температура
imam temperatoora

I'm ... months pregnant
Бременна съм в ... месец
bremnna sum v ... mesrts

I need a prescription for …
Имам нужда от рецепта за ...
imam noozhda ot retsepta za

Can you take these if you're pregnant/breastfeeding?
Може ли да се пие при бременност/кърмене?
mozheh li da seh pieh pri bremennost/kurmeneh

I normally take …
Обикновено вземам ...
obviknoveno vzemam

I'm allergic to …
Имам алергия към ...
imam alergiya kum

Have you got anything for …?
Имате ли нещо за ...?
imateh li neshto za

Do I need a prescription for …?
Трябва ли рецепта за ...?
tryabva li retsepta za

I have lost a filling
Падна ми пломбата
padna mi plombata

THINGS YOU'LL SEE

аптека	*apteka*	pharmacy
болница	*bolnitsa*	hospital
бърза помощ	*burza pomosht*	ambulance
дежурна аптека	*dezhoorna apteka*	pharmacy on duty
зъболекар	*zubolekar*	dentist
кабинет	*kabinet*	surgery
клиника	*klinika*	clinic
лекар	*lekar*	doctor

→

на празен стомах	*na prazen stomaн*	on an empty stomach
оптик	*optik*	optician
поликлиника	*poliklinika*	hospital outpatients
рентгенология	*rentgenologiya*	X-ray department
рецепта	*retsepta*	prescription
спешни случаи	*speshni sloochai*	emergencies; emergency room
уши-нос-гърло	*ooshi-nos-gurlo*	ear, nose, and throat department

THINGS YOU'LL HEAR

po ... tabletki na ... chasa
Take ... pills every ... hours

zvoda
With water

da seh zdufchat
Chew them

edin/dva/tri puti na den
Once/twice/three times a day

samo predi lyaganeh
Only when you go to bed

kakvo vzemateh obiknoveno?
What do you normally take?

tryabva da otideteh na lekar
I think you should see a doctor

suzhalyavam, no tova go nyamameh
I'm sorry, we don't have that

za tova tryabva retsepta
You need a prescription for that

CONVERSION TABLES

DISTANCES

A mile is 1.6km. To convert kilometers to miles, divide the km by 8 and multiply by 5. Convert miles to km by dividing the miles by 5 and multiplying by 8.

miles	0.62	1.24	1.86	2.43	3.11	3.73	4.35	6.21
miles *or* **km**	**1**	**2**	**3**	**4**	**5**	**6**	**7**	**10**
km	1.61	3.22	4.83	6.44	8.05	9.66	11.27	16.10

WEIGHTS

The kilogram is equivalent to 2 lb 3oz. To convert kg to lbs, divide by 5 and multiply by 11. One ounce is about 28 grams, and eight ounces about 227 grams; 1 lb is therefore about 454 grams.

lbs	2.20	4.41	6.61	8.82	11.02	13.23	19.84	22.04
lbs *or* **kg**	**1**	**2**	**3**	**4**	**5**	**6**	**9**	**10**
kg	0.45	0.91	1.36	1.81	2.27	2.72	4.08	4.53

TEMPERATURE

To convert Celsius degrees into Fahrenheit, the accurate method is to multiply the C° figure by 1.8 and add 32. Similarly, to convert F° to C°, subtract 32 from the F° figure and divide by 1.8.

C°	-10	0	5	10	20	30	36.9	40	100
F°	14	32	41	50	68	86	98.4	104	212

LIQUIDS

A liter is about 2.1 pints; a gallon is roughly 3.8 liters.

gals	0.27	0.53	1.33	2.65	5.31	7.96	13.26
gals *or* **liters**	**1**	**2**	**5**	**10**	**20**	**30**	**50**
liters	3.77	7.54	18.85	37.70	75.40	113.10	188.50

TIRE PRESSURES

lb/sq in	18	20	22	24	26	28	30	33
kg/sq cm	1.3	1.4	1.5	1.7	1.8	2.0	2.1	2.3

MINI-DICTIONARY

a *see page 6*
about: about 16 okolo shesnıset
accelerator pedal za gasta
accident zlopolooka
  (*car*) katastrofa
accommodations nastanyavaneh
ache bolka
across: across the street ot droogata
  strana na putya eh
adaptor (*electrical*) adaptor
address adres
adhesive lepilo
adhesive tape lepenka, skoch
after slet
aftershave odekolon za slet brusneneh
again otnovo
against protif, sreshtoo
AIDS SPIN
air (*noun*) vuzdooн
air conditioning
  klimatıchna instalatsiya
aircraft samolet
airline aviokompaniya
airport letishteh
airport bus aftoboos za letishteto
aisle puteka
alarm clock boodilnik
alcohol alkoнol
all fsıchki
  all the streets fsıchki oolitsi
  that's all, thanks
  tova eh fsıchko, blagodarya
almost pochtı
alone sam
already vecheh
always vınagi
am: I am as sum
ambulance linayka
America amerika
106

American (*man*) amerikanets
  (*woman*) amerikanka
  (*adj.*) amerikanski
and i
ankle glezen
another (*different*) drook
  (*one more*) oshteh edin
  another room drooda stıa
  another cup of coffee, please
  oshteh edno kafeн, molya
answering machine telefonen sekretar
antifreeze antifris
antiques shop antikvaren magazin
antiseptic antiseptıchno sretstvo
apartment apartament
aperitif aperitif
appetite apetıt
apple yabulka
application form molba
appointment (*business*) sreshta
  (*at hair salon*) chas
apricot kısiya
are: you are vıeh steh
  (*singular, familiar*) ti si
  we are njeh smeh
  they are teh sa
arm ruka
arrive pristigam
art iskoostvo
art gallery нoodozhestvena galeriya
artist нoodozhnik
as: as soon as possible
  kolkoto seh mozheh po skoro
ashtray pepelnik
asleep: he's asleep toy eh zaspal
aspirin aspirin
at: at the post office fposhtata
  at night prez noshta
  at 3 o'clock ftri chasa

ATM bankomat
attractive privlekatelen
aunt lelya
Australia afstraliya
Australian (man) afstraliyets
  (woman) afstraleeka
  (adj.) afstraleeski
automatic aftomatichen
away: is it far away? dalecheh li eh?
  go away! ostaveteh meh namira!
awful oozhasen
axle os

baby bebeh
baby carriage detska kolichka
baby wipes bebeshki salfetki
back (not front) otzat
  (of body) grup
  to come back vrushtam seh
backpack ranitsa
bacon bekon, poosheni gurdi
bad losh
bag torbichka
  (handbag) chanta
baggage claim poloochavaneh na bagash
bagpipes gida
bait struf
bake peka
baker's foorna
balcony balkon
Balkans balkanskiteh strani
ball topka
ballpoint pen Himikalka
banana banan
band (musicians) orkestur
bandage prevruska
  (adhesive, for cut) laykoplast
bangs (hair) breton
bank banka
bar (for drinks) bar
  bar of chocolate parcheh shokolat
barbecue pecheneh na meso na otkrito
barber's brusnarski salon
bargain izgodna pokoopka

basement sooteren
basket koshnitsa
bath (tub) vana
  to take a bath vzemam vana
baths: public baths opshtestvena banya
bathroom banya, toaletna
battery bateriya
bazaar pazar
beach plash
beans bop
beard brada
beautiful krasif
because zashtoto
bed leglo
bed linen spalno belyo
bedroom spalnya, stja
beef govezhdo
beer bira
before ... predi ...
beginner nachinaesht
beginners' slope pista za nachinaeshti
behind ... zat ...
beige bezhof
below ... doloo ...
belt kolan
beside do
best nidobur
better podobur
between ... mezhdoo ...
bicycle velosipet
big golyam
bikini bikini
bill (money) banknota
bird ptitsa
birthday rozhden den
  happy birthday! chestit rozhden den!
birthday card pozdravitelna kartichka
  za rozhden den
birthday present podaruk za rozhden den
bite (noun) ooHapvaneh
  (verb) Hapya
bitter gorchif
black cheren
blackberry kupina

blackcurrant kasis
Black Sea cherno moreh
blanket odehyalo
bleach (noun) belina
blind (cannot see) slyap
blinds shtori
blister prishka
blizzard vielitsa
blond(e) (adj.) roos
blood kruf
blouse blooza
blue sin
boat korap
    (small) lotka
body tyalo
boil (verb) varya
boiler boyler
bolt (noun: on door) rezeh
    (verb) zalostvam
bone kost
book (noun) kniga
    (verb) zapazvam
bookstore knizharnitsa
boot botoosh
border granitsa
boring skoochen
born: I was born in … roden sum vuf …
both idveteh (f) idvamata (m)
    both of us idvamata
    both … and …
    i … i …
bottle bootilka
bottle opener otvarachka za bootilki
bottom duno
    (part of body) doopeh
bowl panitsa
box kootiya
box office kasa
boy momcheh
boyfriend priyatel
bra sootien
bracelet grivna
brake (noun) spirachka
    (verb) spiram

brandy brendi
bread Hlyap
breakdown (car) povreda
    I've had a breakdown
    kolata mi seh povredi
breakfast zakooska
breathe disham
bridge most
    (game) brich
briefcase diplomatichesko
    koofarcheh
British britanski
brochure broshoora
broiler skara, gril
broken schoopen
    broken leg schoopen krak
brooch broshka
brother brat
brown kafyaf
bruise naturtvaneh
brush (noun) chetka
    (verb: hair) chetkam
    (floor) meta
bucket kofa
building zgrada
Bulgaria bulgariya
Bulgarian (man) bulgarin
    (woman) bulgarka
    (adj.) bulgarski
    the Bulgarians bulgariteh
bumper bronya
burglar kradets
burn (noun) izgaryaneh
    (verb) gorya
bus aftoboos
business biznes
    it's none of your business
    neh eh tvoya rabota
bus station aftogara
busy (occupied) zaeto
    (crowded) ozhiven
but no
butcher's mesarnitsa
butter maslo

button kopcheh
buy koopoovam
by: by the window do prozoretsa
  by Friday do petuk
  by myself sam
  written by … ot …

cabbage zeleh
cabinet shkaf
cable car zakrit lift
cable TV kabelna televiziya
café kafeh-slatkarnitsa
cake torta, pasta
calculator kalkoolator
call: what's it called? kak seh kazva?
camcorder videocamera
camera foto-aparat
camper (RV) karavan
campsite kumpink
camshaft raspredelitelen val
canal kanal
can (tin) konserva
can: can I have …?
  bihteh li mi dali …?
  can you …? mozheteh li …?
  (familiar) mozhesh li …?
Canada kanada
Canadian (man) kanadets
  (woman) kanatka
  (adj.) kanatski
candle svesht
candy bonbon
canoe kanoo
cap (bottle) kapachka
  (hat) kasket
car leka kola
  (train) vagon, putnicheski vagon
carbonated gaziran
carburetor karboorator
card karta
cardigan zhiletka
careful vnimatelen
  be careful! vnimavi!
caretaker oorednik

carpet kilim
carrot morkof
car seat (for a baby)
  bebeshka sedalka za kola
case (suitcase) koofar
cash (noun) pari
  (verb) osrebryavam
  to pay cash plashtam vbroy
cassette kaseta
cassette player kasetofon
castle zamuk
cat kotka
cathedral katedrala
cauliflower karfiol
cave peshtera
cemetery grobishteh
center tsentur
central heating parno
certificate dokooment, svidetelstvo
chair stol
change (noun: money) drebni
  (verb: money) obmenyam
  (clothes) smenyam
check chek
  (in restaurant) smetka
checkbook chekova knishka
check card chekova karta
check-in (desk) registratsiya nabagazha
cheers! (toast) nazdraveh!
cheese sireneh
cherry cheresha
chess shah
chest (part of body) gurdi
chewing gum dufka
chicken pileh
child deteh
children detsa
china portselan
chocolate shokolat
  box of chocolates
  kootiya shokoladovi bonboni
choir hor
chop (food) purzhola, kotlet
  (verb: cut) seka

church tsurkva
cigar poora
cigarette tsigara
cinema kino
city grat
city center gratski tsentur
class klasa
classical music klasicheska moozika
clean (adj.) chist
clear (obvious) yasen
  (water) bistra
clever oomen
clock chasovnik
close (near) blizo
  (stuffy) zadooshen
  (verb) zatvaryam
closed zatvoren, zakrit
clothes dreHi
clutch ambrehash
coat palto
coat hanger zakachalka
cockroach Hlebarka
coffee kafeh
coin moneta
cold (illness) nastinka
  (adj.) stooden
  I have a cold nastinal sum
  I am cold stoodeno mi eh
collar yaka
collection (stamps, etc.) kolektsiya
  (postal) subiraneh na pismata
color tsvyat
color film tsveten film
comb (noun) greben
  (verb) resha seh
come ela
  I come from … as sum ot …
  we came last week
    njeh pristignaHmeh minalata sedmitsa
  come here! ela took!
comforter yoorgan
communist (adj.) komoonisticheski
compact disc kompakten disk
compartment koopeh
110

complicated slozhen
computer kompyootur
concert kontsert
conditioner (for hair) balsam
condom prezervatif
congratulations! chestito!
consulate konsoolstvo
contact lenses kontaktni leshti
contraceptive
  protivozachatuchno sretstvo
cook (noun) gotvach
  (verb) gotvya
cookie biskvita
cooking utensils gotvarski posobiya
cool Hladen
cork tapa
corkscrew tirbooshon
corner ugul
corridor koridor
cosmetics kozmetichni sretstva
cost (verb) tsena, stoynost
  what does it cost? kolko stroova?
cotton pamook
cotton balls meditsinski pamook
cough (noun) kashlitsa
  (verb) kashlyam
cough drops bonboni za gurlo
country (state) durzhava
  (not town) provintsiya
cousin (male) bratofchet
  (female) bratofchetka
crab rak
cramp sHvashtaneh
crayfish omar
cream smetana
credit card kreditna karta
crowded navalitsa
cruise krooiz
crutches pateritsi
cry (weep) placha
  (shout) vikam
cucumber krastavitsa
cuff links kopcheta za rukaveli
cup chasha

curtain zavesa
Customs mitnitsa
cut (noun) poryazvaneh
  (verb: something) rezha
  to cut oneself poryazvam seh

dad tatko
damp vlazhen
dance (noun) tants
  (verb) tantsoovam
dangerous opasen
dark tumen
date data
daughter dushterya
day den
dead murtuf
deaf glooн
dear (person) drak, mil
deck chair shezlonk
deck of cards koloda karti
deep dulbok
delayed zakusnyal
deliberately narochno
dentist zubolekar
deodorant dezodorant
department store ooniversalen magazin
departure zaminavaneh
departure lounge zala zaminavaneh
develop (film) proyavyavam
diamond (jewel) diamant
diaper pelenka
diary dnevnik
dictionary rechnik
die oomiram
different razlichen
  that's different! tova eh neshto novo!
  I'd like a different one
  molya, diteh mi drook
difficult trooden
dining room trapezariya
dirty mrusen
disabled invalit
dishcloth kurpa za sudoveh
dishwashing detergent vero

disposable diapers pelenki, 'Pampers®'
distributor (in car) raspredelitel
dive (verb) gmoorkam seh
divorced (man) razveden
  (woman) razvedena
do pravya
  how do you do? zdravayteh
  (familiar) zdravay
dock kay
doctor lekar
document dokooment
dog koocheh
doll kookla
dollar dolar
door vrata
double room stja zdveh legla
doughnut ponichka
down doloo
dress roklya
drink (noun) napitka
  (verb) pi-ya
  would you like a drink?
  iskash li neshto za pi-eneh?
drinking water voda za pi-eneh
drive (verb) kormoovam
driver shofyor
driver's license shofyorska knishka
drunk piyan
dry sooн
dry-cleaner's Himichesko chisteneh
during po vremeh na
dust cloth partsal za praн

each (every) fseki
  twenty leva each po dvjset leva
ear ooнo
early rano
earrings obetsi
east istok
easy lesen
eat yam
egg yitseh
either: either of them koyto idaeн
  either ... or ... ili ... ili ...

elastic elastichen
elbow lakut
electric elektricheski
electricity elektrichestvo
elevator asansyor
else: something else neshto droogo
  someone else nyakoy drook
  somewhere else
  nyakudeh droogadeh
email imayl
email address imayl adres
embarrassing smooshtavasht
embassy posolstvo
embroidery broderiya
emergency speshen sloochı
emergency brake
  (train) vnezapna spirachka
emergency exit pozharen isHot
empty prazen
end krı
engaged (couple) zgodeni
engine (motor) dvigatel
England angliya
English (adj.) angleeski
  (language) angleeski ezık
Englishman anglichanin
Englishwoman anglichanka
enlargement oogolemyavaneh
enough dostatuchno
entertainment razvlechenieh
entrance fHot
envelope plik
eraser goomichka
escalator eskalator
especially osobeno
evening vecher
every fseki
everyone fsichki
everything fsichko
everywhere nafsyakudeh
example primer
  for example naprimer
excellent choodesen
excess baggage svruHbagash

exchange (verb) obmenyam
exchange rate obmenen koors
excursion exkoorziya
excuse me! izvineteh!
  (pardon) izvinyaviteh!
excuse me? molya?
exit isHot
expensive skup
extension cord kabelen oodulzhitel
eye oko
  eyes ochı

face litseh
faint (unclear) bleden
  (verb) pripadam
fair (noun) panair
  it's not fair neh eh chestno
false teeth iskoostveni zubi
family semaystvo
fan (ventilator) ventilator
  (soccer) zapalyanko
  (pop, etc.) pochitatel
fan belt remuk na oHlazhdaneto
fantastic fantastichen
far daleko
  how far is it to …?
  kolko eh daleko do …?
fare tsena na bilet
farm selsko stopanstvo
farmer zemedelets
fashion moda
fast burs
fat (person) debel
  (on meat, etc.) maznina
father bashta
faucet kran
fax (noun) telefax
  (verb) izprashtam telefax
fax machine faks
feel (touch) choofstvam
  I feel hot goreshto mi eh
  I feel like … iskamiseh da …
feel: I don't feel well
  neh seh choofstvam dobreh

112

feet kraka

felt-tip pen foolmaster

fence ograda

ferry *(small)* lotka
   (large) feribot

fever treska

fiancé godenik

fiancée godenitsa

field poleh

filling *(in tooth)* plomba
   (in sandwich, cake, etc.) pulnesh

film film

filter filtur

finger prust

fire ogun
   (blaze) pozhar

fire extinguisher pozharogasitel

fireworks foyerverki

first pruf

first aid purva pomosht

first floor parter

first name malko imeh

fish riba

fishing ribolof
   to go fishing otivam na ribolof

fishing rod vuditsa

fish market ribarski magazin

flag znameh

flash *(camera)* svetkavitsa

flashlight fenercheh

flat *(level)* plosuk

flavor fkoos

flea bulHa

flight polet

flippers plavnitsi

floor pot
   (story) etash

flour brashno

flower tsveteh

fly *(insect)* mooHa
   (verb) letya

fog mugla

folk dancing narodni tantsi

folklore folklor

folk music narodna moozika

food Hrana

food poisoning
   Hranitelno otravyaneh

foot krak

for za
   for me za meneh
   what for? za kakvo?
   for a week za edna sedmitsa

foreigner choozhdenets

forest gora

forget zabravyam

fork vilitsa

fortress krepost

fourth chetvurti

free *(not busy)* svoboden
   (no charge) besplaten

freezer frizer

French frenski

french fries purzheni kartofi

friend priyatel

friendly priyatelski

front: in front of … pret …

frost mras

fruit plot

fruit juice plodof sok

fry purzha

frying pan tigan

full pulen
   I'm full (up) nayadoH seh

full board pulen pansion

funny smeshen
   (odd) stranen

furniture mebeli

garage garash

garbage smet, boklook

garbage can kofa za smet

garbage can liner torba za boklook

garden gradina

garlic chesun

gas benzin

gas-permeable lenses
   gazopronitsaemi leshti

113

gas station benzinostantsiya
gate porta
   (at airport) isHot
gear *(of car)* skorost
gearshift ruchka za skorostiteh
gel *(for hair)* gel
German *(adj.)* germanski,
   nemski
get *(fetch, catch)* vzemam
   have you got …? imash li …?
   to get the train vzemam vlaka
get back: we get back tomorrow
   ootreh seh vrushtameh
   to get something back vuzvrushtam si
get in vlizam
   (arrive) pristigam
get off *(bus, etc.)* slizam
get on *(bus, etc.)* kachvam seh
get out izlizam
get up *(rise)* stavam
gift podaruk
gin jin
girl momicheh
girlfriend priyatelka
give davam
glad dovolen
glass *(material)* stuklo
   (for drinking) chasha
glasses ochila
gloss prints glantsirani snimki
gloves rukavitsi
glue lepilo
go otivam
gold zlato
good dobur
   good! dobreh!
goodbye dovizhdaneh
gorge prolom
government pravitelstvo
granddaughter vnoochka
grandfather dyado
grandmother baba
grandparents dyado i baba
grandson vnook

grapes grozdeh
grass treva
gray sif
Great Britain velikobritaniya
Greece gurtsi-ya
Greek *(adj.)* grutski
   (man) gruk
   (woman) gurkinya
green zelen
grocery Hranitelni stoki
groundcloth platnishteh
guarantee *(noun)* garantsiya
   (verb) garantiram
guard *(on train)* kondooktor
guide exkoorzovot
guidebook putevoditel
guitar kitara
gun *(rifle)* pooshka
   (pistol) pistolet

hair kosa
haircut potstrigvaneh
hair dryer seshwar
hair salon *(men's)* brusnarski salon
   (women's) frizyorski salon
hair spray lak za kosa
half polovina
   half an hour polovin chas
half board poloo pansion
ham shoonka
hamburger Hamboorger
hammer chook
hand ruka
handbag damska chanta
handbrake ruchna spirachka
handle *(of door)* drushka
handsome Hoobaf
hangover maHmoorlook
happy shtastlif
harbor pristanishteh
hard tvurt
   (difficult) trooden
hardware store magazin za domashni
   protrebi izhelezariya

hat shapka

have imam
  I don't have ... nyamam ...
  have you got ...? imateh li ...?

hay fever senna нrema

he toy

head glava

headache glavobolieh

headlights faroveh

hear choovam

hearing aid slooнof aparat

heart surtseh

heater pechka, otoplitelen ooret

heating otoplenieh

heavy tezhuk

heel (of foot) peta
  (of shoe) tok

hello zdravay
  (on phone) alo

help (noun) pomosht
  (verb) pomagam

hepatitis hepatit

her: **it's her** tya eh
  it's for her za nehya eh
  give it to her di-i go
  her apartment nayniya apartament
  her book naynata kniga
  her name naynoto imeh
  her shoes nayniteh oboofki
  it's hers nayno eh

hi! zdrasti!

high visok

highway aftomagistrala

hill нulm

him: **it's him** toy eh
  it's for him za nego eh
  give it to him di moo go

his: **his apartment** negoviya apartament
  his book negovata kniga
  his name negovoto imeh
  his shoes negoviteh oboofki
  it's his negovo eh

history istoriya

hitchhike dvizha seh na aftostop

HIV positive HIV pozitiven (m) /
  HIV pozitivna (f)

hobby нobi

home: **at home** fkushti

homosexual нomosexooalist

honest chesten

honey met

honeymoon meden mesets

hood (car) kapak

horn (of car) klakson
  (of animal) rok

horrible oozhasen

hospital bolnitsa

hot-water bottle grayka

hour chas

house kushta

how? kak?

hungry: **I'm hungry** gladen sum

hurry: **I'm in a hurry** burzam

husband suprook

I as

ice let

ice cream sladolet

ice skates kunki za let

ice-skating: **to go ice-skating**
  karam kunki na let

icon ikon

if ako

ignition zapalvaneh

ill bolen

immediately vednaga

impossible nevuzmozhen

in v
  in English na angleeski
  in the hotel fнotela
  in Sofia fsofia

indicator pokazatel

indigestion stomashno rastroystvo

inexpensive eftin

infection infektsiya

information informatsiya

injection inzhektsiya

injury naranyavaneh

115

ink mastilo
inn Han
inner tube vutreshna gooma
insect nasekomo
insect repellent sretstvo protif nasekomi
insomnia bessunieh
instant coffee neskafeh
insurance zastraHofka
interesting interesen
internet internet
interpret prevezhdam oostno
interpreter prevodach
invitation pokana
Ireland irlandiya
Irish irlantski
Irishman irlandets
Irishwoman irlantka
iron (*material*) zhelyazo
    (*for clothes*) yootiya
    (*verb*) gladya
is: he/she/it is … toy/tya/to eh …
island ostrof
it to
its negof

jacket yakeh
    (*of suit*) sako
jam konfityoor, slatko
jazz jas
jeans jinsi, dunki
jellyfish medooza
jeweler's bizhooteriya
job rabota, zanimanieh *
jog (*verb*) ticham za zdraveh
    to go for a jog izlizam da ticham
jogging suit antsook iklin
joke shega
just (*only*) samo
    I've just one left
    ostanal mi eh samo edin
    it's just arrived tokoo shto pristigna

kettle chinik
key klyooch

kidney bubrek
kilo kilo, kilogram
kilometer kilometur
kitchen kooHnya
knee kolyano
knife nosh
knit pleta
knitwear trikotash
know: I don't know neh znaya

label etiket
lace dantela
laces (*of shoe*) vruski
lady dama, zhena
lake ezero
lamb (*meat*) agneshko
lamp lampa
lampshade abazhoor
land (*noun*) zemya
    (*verb*) katsam
language ezik
large golyam
last (*final*) posleden
    last week minalata sedmitsa
    at last! ni posleh!
last name familno imeh
late zakusnyal
    the bus is late
    aftoboosa ima zakusnenieh
later po-kusno
laugh (*noun*) smyaH
laundry (*place*) peralnya
    (*dirty clothes*) praneh
laundry detergent praH za praneh
laxative rasslabitelno sretstvo
lazy murzelif
leaf list
leaflet broshoora
learn oocha
leather kozha
left (*not right*) lyaf
    there's nothing left
    nishto neh eh ostanalo
leg krak

lemon limon
lemonade limonada
length dulzhina
lens leshta
  (of camera) obektif
less po malko
lesson oorok
letter pismo
  (of alphabet) bookva
letter carrier poshtajiya
lettuce maroolya
library biblioteka
license razreshitelno
license plate registratsionen nomer
life zhivot
lift: could you give me a lift?
  shte meh otkarash li skolata?
light *(noun)* svetni lampata
  (adj.: not heavy) lek
  (not dark) svetul
light bulb krooshka
light meter svetlomer
lighter zapalka
lighter fluid gorivo za raspalvaneh
like: I like you Haresvam teh
  I like swimming
  obicham da ploovam
  it's like …
  kato … eh
  like this one
  kato tozi
line *(of people, cars, etc.)* opashka
  (to wait in line) redya se na opashka
lip balm meHlem za oosni
lipstick chervilo
liqueur likyor
list spisuk
liter litur
litter boklook
little *(small)* maluk
  it's a little big malko eh golyam
  just a little sufsem malko
liver cheren drop
lollipop karamel na klechka

long duluk
lost and found office
  byooro za izgoobeni veshti
lot: a lot mnogo
loud silen
  (color) yaruk
lounge fwa-eh
love *(noun)* lyoobof, obich
  (verb) obicham
low nisuk
  (voice) tiH
luck kusmet
  good luck! nadobur chas!
luggage bagash
luggage rack bagazhnik
luggage storage locker kabini za bagash
luggage storage office garderop
lunch obyat

mad loot
magazine spisanieh
mail poshta
  (verb) prashtam po poshtata
mailbox poshtenska kootiya
make pravya
makeup grim
man mush
manager *(in hotel, etc.)* oopravitel
many: not many neh mnogo
map karta
  a map of Sofia
  karta na sofia
marble mramor
margarine margarin
market pazar
marmalade marmalat
married *(man)* zhenen
  (woman) omuzhena
mascara spirala
mass *(church)* sloozhba
mast machta
match *(light)* klechka kibrit
  (sports) mach
material *(cloth)* plat

matter: it doesn't matter
  nyama znachenieh
mattress dyooshek
maybe mozheh bi
me: it's me as sum
  it's for me za meneh eh
  give it to me di mi go
meal yadenieh
mean: what does this mean?
  kakvo znachi tova?
meat meso
mechanic meнanik
medicine lekarstvo
medium (steak) sredno opechena
medium-sized sreden rust
meeting sreshta
melon pupesh
men's restroom muzheh
menu menyoo
message suopshtenieh
middle: in the middle fsredata
midnight poloonosht
milk mlyako
mine: it's mine moeh eh
mineral water mineralna voda
minute minoota
mirror ogledalo
Miss gospozhitsa
mistake greshka
mobile phone mobifon
modem modem
mom mama
monastery manastir
money pari
month mesets
monument pametnik
moon loona
moped motopet
more oshteh
morning sootrin
  in the morning sootrinta
mosaic mozika
mosque jamiya
mosquito komar
118

mother mlka
motorboat kater, motorna lotka
motorcycle mototsiklet
mountain planina
mountain pass planinski proнot
mouse mishka
mousse (for hair) moos za kosa
mouth oosta
move: please move your car
  biнteh li si premestili kolata?
  don't move! neh murdi!
Mr. gospodin
Mrs. gospozha
mug chasha zdrushka
mural stenopis
museum moozay
mushroom guba
music moozika
musical instrument
  moozikalen instrooment
musician moozikant
mussels midi
must: I must … tryabva da …
mustache moostatsi
mustard gorchitsa
my: my apartment moya apartament
  my handbag moyata chanta
  my name moeto imeh
  my keys moiteh klyoochoveh

nail (metal) gvozday
  (finger) nokut
nail clippers rezachka za nokti
nailfile pila za nokti
nail polish lak za nokti
name imeh
  what's your name?
  kak seh kazvash?
napkin salfetka
narrow tesen
near … blizo do …
necessary noozhno
neck vrat
necklace gerdan

need (verb) noozhd**a**ya seh
  I need ... imam no**o**zhda ot ...
  there's no need ny**a**ma n**o**ozhda
needle igl**a**
negative (noun) negat**i**f
neither: neither of them
  n**i**to ed**i**n ot tyaн
  neither ... nor ...
  n**i**to ... n**i**to ...
nephew pl**e**mennik
never n**i**koga
new nof
news nov**i**ni
newspaper v**e**snik
newsstand rep
New Zealand n**o**va zel**a**ndiya
New Zealander (man) novozel**a**ndets
  (woman) novozel**a**ntka
next sl**e**dvasht
  next week sl**e**dvashtata s**e**dmitsa
  what next? kakv**o** **o**shteh?
nice (attractive) н**oo**baf
  (pleasant) priy**a**ten
  (to eat) fk**oo**sen
niece pl**e**mennitsa
night nosht
nightclub n**o**shten bar
nightgown vech**e**rno obl**e**klo
night porter n**o**shten port**ie**r
no (response) neh
  no ... nikakuf ...
  I have no money ny**a**mam par**i**
noisy sh**oo**men
noon **o**bet
north s**e**ver
Northern Ireland s**e**verna irl**a**ndi-ya
nose nos
not neh
  he's not ... toy neh eh ...
notebook bel**e**zhnik
nothing n**i**shto
novel rom**a**n
now se**ga**
nowhere n**i**kudeh

number n**o**mer
nut (fruit) y**a**tka
  (for bolt) g**i**ka

occasionally pony**a**koga
occupied za**e**to
of na
office kant**o**ra, kantsel**a**riya
often ch**e**sto
oil masl**o**
ointment мeн**le**m
OK d**o**breh
old star
  how old are you?
  na k**o**lko si g**o**dini?
olive masl**i**na
omelette oml**e**t
on ... vurн**oo** ...
one ed**i**n
onion look
only s**a**mo
open (verb) otv**a**ryam
  (adj.) otv**o**ren
operation oper**a**tsiya
operator (man) telef**o**nist
  (woman) telef**o**nistka
opposite: opposite the hotel
  sresht**oo** н**o**tela
optician opt**i**k
or il**i**
orange (color) or**a**nzhef
  (fruit) portok**a**l
orange juice portok**a**lof sok
orchestra ork**e**stur
ordinary obikn**o**ven
Orthodox pravosl**a**ven
other: the other ...
  dr**oo**giya ...
our nash
  it's ours n**a**sheh eh
out vun
  he's out n**e**go go ny**a**ma
outside nav**u**n
oven f**oo**rna, gotv**a**rska p**e**chka

119

over *(more than)* nat
  (finished) kri
over: over there ay tam

pacifier *(for baby)* biberon
package *(parcel)* paket, kolet
packet: a packet of ... paket ...
padlock katinar
page stranitsa
pain bolka
painkiller analgin®
paint *(noun)* boya
pair chift
pajamas pizhama
palace dvorets
pale blet
pants pantaloni
pantyhose chorapogashti
paper Hartiya
  (newspaper) vesnik
paraffin kerosin
parents roditeli
park *(noun)* park
  (verb) parkiram
parking lights stranichni svetlini
part *(in hair)* put
party *(celebration)* gosti, subiraneh
  (group) kompaniya
  (political) partiya
pass *(driving)* isprevarvam
passenger putnik
passport pasport
pasta makaroni
pastry shop slatkarnitsa
path puteka
pay plashtam
peach praskova
peanuts fustutsi
pear kroosha
pearl perla
peas graH
pedestrian pesheHodets
pen pisalka
pencil molif
120

pencil sharpener ostrilka
people Hora
pepper piper
per: per night na nosht
perfect ideh-alen
perfume parfyoom
perhaps mozheh bi
perm kudreneh
personal stereo wokman
pharmacy apteka
phone book ookazatel
phonecard telefonna karta
photocopier kseroks
photograph *(noun)* snimka
  (verb) snimam, fotografiram
photographer fotograf
phrase book razgovornik
piano piano
pickpocket kradets
picnic piknik
piece parcheh
pill tabletka
pillow vuzglavnitsa
pin topleeka
  (for clothes) shtipka
pineapple ananas
pink rozof
pipe *(for smoking)* loola
  (for water) truba
Pirin Mountains pirin planina
piston bootalo
pizza pitsa
place myasto
  at your place oovas
plant rastenieh
plastic *(adj.)* plasmasof
plastic bag nilonof plik
plate chiniya
platform peron
play *(theater)* piesa
  (verb) igraya
please molya
plug *(electrical)* shtepsel
  (for sink) zapooshalka

pocket jop
pocketknife jobno noshcheh
poison otrova
police politsiya
police officer politsi
police station politsayski oochastuk
poor beden
  (bad) losh
pop music pop moozika
pork svinsko meso
port (harbor) pristanishteh
  (drink) port
porter (hotel) portier
possible vuzmozhen
postcard poshtenska kartichka
poster afish, plakat
post office poshta
potato kartof
potato chips chips
poultry (meat) pileshko meso
pound (weight) foont
  (money) lira sterlinga
powder (medicine) praн
  (for face) poodra
prefer pretpochitam
prescription retsepta
pretty (beautiful) ноobaf
  (quite) dosta
  pretty good dosta
priest dosta dobur
private chasten
problem problem
public opshtestven
pull durpam
puncture spookvaneh na gooma
purple moraf
purse portmoneh
push bootam
put slagam

quality kachestvo
quarter chetvurt
question vupros
quick burs

quiet tiн
quite (fairly) dosta
  (fully) sufsem

radiator radiator
radio radio
radish repichka
railroad zhelezoputna liniya
rain dusht
rainboots goomeni botooshi
raincoat duzhdobran
raisins stafidi
raspberry malina
rare (uncommon) ryaduk
  (steak) nedopechen
rat pluн
razor blades noshcheta za brusneneh
read cheta
ready gotof
receipt kvitantsiya
receptionist (man) administrator
  (woman) administratorka
record (music) gramofonna plocha
  (sports, etc.) rekort
record store magazin za plochi
red cherven
  (hair) rizha
refreshments zakooski
refrigerator нladilnik
registered letter preporuchano pismo
relative rodnina
relax otpooskam seh
religion religiya
remember pomnya
  I remember spomnyam si
  I don't remember neh si spomnyam
rent (verb) naemam
  for rent pod naem
reservation rezervatsiya
rest (noun: remainder) ostatuk
  (verb: relax) pochivam si
restaurant restorant
return (come back) vrushtam seh
  (give back) vrushtam

rice or<u>i</u>s

rich bog<u>a</u>t

right *(correct)* pr<u>a</u>vilen

   (not left) d<u>e</u>sen

Rila Mountains r<u>i</u>la plan<u>i</u>na

ring *(jewelry)* pr<u>u</u>sten

ripe zry<u>a</u>l

river r<u>e</u>ka

road put

rock *(stone)* k<u>a</u>muk

   (music) rok

roll *(bread)* нl<u>e</u>pcheh

Romania room<u>u</u>nia

Romanian room<u>u</u>nski

   (man) room<u>u</u>nets

   (woman) room<u>u</u>nka

roof p<u>o</u>krif

room st<u>i</u>a

   (space) my<u>a</u>sto

rope vuzh<u>e</u>h

rose r<u>o</u>za

round *(circular)* kr<u>u</u>gul

   it's my round moy ret eh

round-trip ticket

   bil<u>e</u>t za ot<u>i</u>vaneh i vr<u>u</u>shtaneh

rowboat gr<u>e</u>bna l<u>o</u>tka

rubber *(material)* g<u>oo</u>ma

rubber band l<u>a</u>stik

ruby *(stone)* roob<u>i</u>n

rug *(mat)* kil<u>i</u>mcheh

ruins razval<u>i</u>ni

ruler *(for drawing)* l<u>i</u>ni-ya

rum rom

run *(verb)* by<u>a</u>gam

sad t<u>u</u>zhen

safe *(not in danger)* bezop<u>a</u>sen

safety pin bezop<u>a</u>sna igl<u>a</u>

sailboat platnoн<u>o</u>tka

salad sal<u>a</u>ta

salami salam 'zak<u>oo</u>ska'®

sale *(at reduced prices)* rasprod<u>a</u>zhba

salmon sy<u>o</u>mga

salt sol

same: the same dress s<u>u</u>shtata r<u>o</u>klya

   same again, please

   <u>o</u>shteh ot s<u>u</u>shtoto, m<u>o</u>lya

sand py<u>a</u>suk

sandals sand<u>a</u>li

sandwich s<u>a</u>ndvich

sanitary napkins d<u>a</u>mski prevr<u>u</u>ski

satellite TV satel<u>i</u>tna televiz<u>i</u>ya

sauce sos

saucepan t<u>e</u>njera

sauna s<u>a</u>oona

sausage sal<u>a</u>m

say k<u>a</u>zvam

   what did you say? kakv<u>o</u> k<u>a</u>za?

   how do you say …? kak da k<u>a</u>zha …?

scarf shalch<u>e</u>h

   (head) k<u>u</u>rpa za glav<u>a</u>

school ooch<u>i</u>lishteh

scissors n<u>o</u>zhitsi

Scotland shotl<u>a</u>ndi-ya

Scotsman shotl<u>a</u>ndets

Scotswoman shotl<u>a</u>ntka

Scottish shotl<u>a</u>ntski

screw vint

screwdriver otv<u>e</u>rka

sea mor<u>e</u>h

seat my<u>a</u>sto

seat belt pretp<u>a</u>zen kol<u>a</u>n

second *(of time)* sek<u>oo</u>nda

   (in series) ft<u>o</u>ri

second floor p<u>u</u>rvi et<u>a</u>sh

see v<u>i</u>zhdam

   I can't see neh m<u>o</u>ga da v<u>i</u>dya

   I see razb<u>i</u>ram

sell prod<u>a</u>vam

send ispr<u>a</u>shtam

separate otd<u>e</u>len

separated otd<u>e</u>len

serious seri<u>o</u>zen

several ny<u>a</u>kolko

sew sh<u>i</u>ya

shampoo shampw<u>a</u>n

shave *(noun)* br<u>u</u>sneneh

   to have a shave br<u>u</u>sna seh

shaving cream pyana za brusneneh
shawl shal
she tya
sheet charshaf
shell cheroopka
sherry sheri
ship korap
shirt riza
shoelaces vruski za oboofki
shoe polish boya za oboofki
shoes oboofki
shoe store magazin za oboofki
shopping pazaroovaneh
  to go shopping pazaroovam
short *(sleeve, etc.)* kus
  (person) nisuk
shorts shorti
shoulder ramo
shower *(bath)* doosh
  (rain) lek dusht
shower gel techen sapoon
shutter *(camera)* zatvor
  (window) kepenk
sick *(ill)* bolen
  I feel sick povrushta mi seh
  to be sick *(vomit)* povrushtam
side *(edge)* strana
sidewalk putna nastilka
sights: the sights of …
  zabelezhitelnostiteh na …
silk koprina
silver *(color)* srebrist
  (metal) srebro
simple prost
sing pehya
single *(one)* edin
  (unmarried: man) nezhenen
  (woman) neomuzhena
single room edinichna stia
sink mifka
sister sestra
skate kunka
skates kunki
ski *(verb)* karam ski

ski binding ski aftomat
ski boots ski oboofki
skid *(verb)* booksoovam
skiing: to go skiing
  otivam da karam ski
ski lift ski lift
skin cleanser losion
ski resort ski koorort
skirt riza
skis ski
ski poles shteki
sky nebeh
sledge shayna
sleep *(noun)* sun
  (verb) spya
  to go to sleep zaspivam
sleeper car spalen vagon
sleeping bag spalen chooval
sleeping pill sunotvorno Hapcheh
slip *(garment)* foosta
slippers cheHli
slow baven
small maluk
smell *(noun)* mirizma
  (verb) mirisha
smile *(noun)* oosmifka
  (verb) oosmiHvam seh
smoke *(noun)* pooshek
  (verb) poosha
snack zakooska
sneakers maratonki
snorkel shnorHel
snow snyak
so: so good tolkova Hoobavo
  not so much neh tolkova mnogo
soaking solution *(for contact lenses)*
  rastvor za kontaktni leshti
soap sapoon
soccer footbol
socks chorapi
soda water gazirana voda, soda
somebody nyakoy
somehow nyakaksi
something neshto

sometimes ponyakoga
somewhere nyakudeh
son sin
song pesen
sorry! *(apology)* izvinyaviteh!
  I'm sorry izvinyaviteh
  sorry? *(pardon)* molya?
soup soopa
south yook
souvenir soovenir
spade lopata
spare parts rezervni chasti
spark plug svesht
speak govorya
  do you speak …? govoriteh li …?
  I don't speak … neh govorya …
speed skorost
speed limit ogranichenieh na skorosta
speedometer spidometur
spider plak
spinach spanach
spoon luzhitsa
sports center sporten tsentur
spring *(mechanical)* proozhina
  (season) prolet
square *(noun: in town)* ploshtat
  (adj.: in shape) kvadrat
stadium stadion
staircase stulbishteh
stairs stulbi
stamp marka
stapler telbot
star zvezda
  (movie) filmova zvezda
start *(noun: beginning)* nachalo
  (verb) trugvam
  (work, etc.) zapochvam
station gara
statue statooya
steak purzhola
steal krada
  it's been stolen otkradnato eh
steamer *(boat)* parahot
steering wheel kormilo
124

sting *(noun)* zhilo
  (verb) zhilya
  it stings shtipeh
stockings damski chorapi
stomach stomah
stomachache bolki fstomaha
stop *(noun: for bus)* spirka
  (verb) spiram
  stop! spreteh!
store magazin
storm boorya
strawberry yagoda
stream *(small river)* roochay
street oolitsa
string *(cord)* vruf
  (of guitar, etc.) stroona
stroller detska sportna kolichka
strong *(person, drink)* silen
  (material) zdraf
student student
stupid tup
suburbs predgradiya
sugar zahar
suit *(noun)* kostyoom
  it suits you otiva ti
suitcase koofar
sun sluntseh
sunbathe peka seh na sluntseh
sunburn slunchevo izgaryaneh
sunglasses ochila za sluntseh
sunny: it's sunny vremeto eh slunchevo
sunshade chadur
suntan: to get a suntan
  pochernyavam ot sluntseto
suntan lotion plazhno mlyako
suntanned pochernyal
supermarket soopermarket
supper vecherya
supplement dobafka
sure sigooren
  are you sure? sigooren li si?
sweat *(noun)* pot
  (verb) potya seh
sweatshirt antsook

sweater poolover
sweet (not sour) sladuk
swim (verb) ploovam
swimming pool plooven basayn
swimming trunks ploofki
swimsuit banski kostyoom
switch klyooch
synagogue sinagoga

table masa
taillights stopoveh
take vzemam
takeoff izlitaneh
takeout (food) Hrana zafkushti
talcum powder talk
talk (noun) razgovor
    (verb) govorya
tall visok
tampons tamponi
tangerine mandarina
tapestry goblen
tea chı
teacher oochitel
telegram telegrama
telephone (noun) telefon
    (verb) obazhdam seh
telephone booth telefonna kabina
telephone call telefonno obazhdaneh
television televiziya
temperature temperatoora
tent palatka
tent pole toyashka za palatka
tent stake kolcheh
than otkolkoto
thank blagodarya
    thank you/thanks blagodarya
that (that one) onova
    that man onzi chovek
    that woman onazi zhena
    that seat onova myasto
    what's that? kakvo eh onova?
    I think that ... mislya, cheh ...
the -ut/-yat (m), -ta (f), -to (n); (plural)
-te (m/f) -ta (n); see pages 5-6

their: their apartment teHniya (m)
    apartament
    their room tyaHnata (f) stia
    their school tyaHnoto (n) oochilishteh
    their books teHniteh (pl) knigi
    it's theirs tyaHno eh
them: it's them teh sa
    it's for them za tyaH eh
    give it to them dı-im go
then togava
    (after) slet tova
there tam
    there is/are ... ima ...
    is/are there ...? ima li ...?
these tezi
they teh
thick debel
thin tunuk
think mislya
    I think so taka mislya
    I'll think about it
    shteh si pomislya
third treti
thirsty: I'm thirsty zhaden sum
this (this one) tova
    this man tozi mush
    this woman tazi zhena
    this seat tova myasto
    what's this? kakvo eh tova?
    this is Mr. ... tova eh gospodin ...
those onezi
throat gurlo
through pres
thumbtack gaburcheh
thunderstorm grumotevichna boorya
ticket bilet
ticket office kasa za bileti
tide prilif
tie (noun) vratovruska
    (verb) vruzvam
tight stegnat
time vremeh
    what's the time? kolko eh chasa?
timetable (train, bus) raspisanieh

tip *(money)* bakshish
  (end) kricheh
tire *(wheel)* aftomobilna gooma
tired izmoren
tissues knizhna kurpichka
to: to America do amerika
  to the station do garata
  to the doctor na lekar
toast prepechen Hlyap
tobacco tyootyoon
toboggan sportna shayna
today dnes
together zaedno
toilet toaletna
toilet paper toaletna Hartiya
tomato domat
tomato juice domaten sok
tomorrow ootreh
tongue ezik
tonic tonik
tonight dovechera
too *(also)* sushto
  (excessively) prekaleno
tooth zup
toothache zubobol
toothbrush chetka za zubi
toothpaste pasta za zubi
tour obikolka
tourist toorist
tourist office tooristichesko byooro
towel Havliya, kurpa
tower koola
town grat
town hall kmetstvo
toy igrachka
toy store magazin za igrachki
tradition traditsiya
traffic dvizhenieh
traffic lights svetofar
trailer remarkeh
train vlak
translate prevezhdam pismeno
translator prevodach
travel agency byooro za toorizum
126

traveler's check putnicheski chek
tray podnos
tree durvo
trip putoovaneh
truck kamion
true veren
trunk *(car)* bagazhnik
try opitvam
tunnel toonel
Turk *(man)* toorchin
  (woman) toorkinya
Turkey toortsiya
Turkish *(adj.)* toorski
tweezers pintseti
typewriter pisheshta mashina

umbrella chadur
uncle *(father's brother)* chicho
  (mother's brother) vooicho
under ... pot ...
underpants dolni gashteta
undershirt potnik
understand razbiram
  I don't understand neh razbiram
underwear belyo
university ooniversitet
unleaded bezoloven
unmarried *(man)* nezhenen
  (woman) neomuzhena
until dokato
unusual neobiknoven
up nagoreh
  up there tam goreh
urgent speshen
us: it's us ni-eh smeh
  it's for us zanas eh
  give it to us diteh ni go
use *(noun)* oopotreba, ispolzvaneh
  (verb) oopotrebyavam, ispolzvam
  it's no use bespolezno eh
useful polezen
usual obiknoven
usually obiknoveno

vacancy (*room*) svobodna stia
vacation praznik
vacuum cleaner praнosmookachka
valley dolina
valve klapa
vanilla vaniliya
vase vaza
veal teleshko
vegetable zelenchook
vegetarian (*noun*) vegetarianets
  (*adj.*) vegetarianski
vehicle prevozno sretstvo
very (*much*) mnogo
video (*tape*) videokaseta
  (*film*) videofilm
video recorder video
view izglet
viewfinder vizyor
villa vila
village selo
vinegar otset
visa viza
visit (*noun: to person*) gostoovaneh
  (*to place*) poseshtenieh
  (*verb: person*) gostoovam na
  (*place*) poseshtavam
visitor (*to museum, etc.*) posetitel
  (*guest*) gost
vitamin pill vitamin
vodka votka
voice glas

wait chakam
  wait! chaki!
waiter servityor
  waiter! izvineteh! kelner!
waiting room chakalnya
waitress servityorka
  waitress! izvineteh! kelner!
Wales Wels
walk (*noun: stroll*) rasнotka
  (*verb*) нodya
  to take a walk otivam na rasнotka
wall stena

wallet portfayl
war voyna
wardrobe garderop
warm topul
was: I was as byaн
  he was toy besheh
  she was tya besheh
  it was to besheh
wasp osa
watch (*wristwatch*) ruchen chasovnik
  (*verb*) nablyoodavam
water voda
waterfall vodopat
water heater nagrevatel za voda
wave (*noun*) vulna
  (*verb: with hand*) maнam
wavy (*hair*) na vulni
we ni-eh
weather vremeh
website ooeb sayt
wedding svadba
week sedmitsa
welcome (*verb*) doshli
  you're welcome molya
Welsh welski
Welshman welsets
were: we were nieh byaнmeh
  you were vieh byaнteh
  (*singular, familiar*) ti besheh
  they were teh byaнa
west zapat
wet mokur
what? kakvo?
wheel kolelo
wheelchair invalidna kolichka
when? koga?
where? kudeh?
whether dali
which? koy?
whiskey wiski
white byal
who? koy?
why? zashto?
wide shirok

wife suprooga, zhena
wind vyatur
window prozorets
windshield predno stuklo
wine vino
wine list menyoo za vinata
wine merchant turgovets na vino
wing krilo
with s
without bes
woman zhena
women's restroom zheni
wood (*material*) durvo
wool vulna
word dooma
work (*noun*) rabota
  (*verb*) rabotya
worse po losho
worst nl losho
wrapping paper Hartiya za oovivaneh, ambalazhna Hartiya
wrench gaechen klyooch
wrist kitka
writing paper listi za pisma
wrong greshen

year godina
yellow zhult
yes da
yesterday fchera
yet: is it ready yet?
  gotovo li eh vecheh?
  not yet neh oshteh
yogurt kiselo mlyako
you vieh
  (*singular, familiar*) ti
your: your friend vashiya (*m*) priyatel
  (*familiar*) tvoya (*m*) priyatel
  your book vashata (*f*) kniga
  (*familiar*) tvoyata (*f*) kniga
  your seat vasheto (*n*) myasto
  (*familiar*) tvoeto (*n*) myasto
  your shoes vashiteh (*pl*) oboofki
  (*familiar*) tvoiteh (*pl*) oboofki
yours: is this yours?
  tova vasheh li eh?
  (*familiar*) tova tvoeh li eh?
youth hostel stoodentsko opshtezhitieh

zipper tsip
zoo zo-ologicheska gradina, zo-opark